KU-190-925

A GUIDE TO THE ORIGIN OF BRITISH SURNAMES

A GUIDE TO THE ORIGIN OF BRITISH SURNAMES

BY

C. L'ESTRANGE EWEN

Author of

"*A History of Surnames of the British Isles,*"
"*Witch Hunting and Witch Trials,*"
"*Lotteries and Sweepstakes,*" "*Witchcraft and Demonianism,*"
etc.

JOHN GIFFORD LIMITED
62 FRITH STREET, LONDON, W.C.2

First published, 1938

MADE AND PRINTED IN GREAT BRITAIN BY
EBENEZER BAYLIS AND SON, LTD., THE
TRINITY PRESS, WORCESTER, AND LONDON

PREFACE

The study of surnames should rank as an educational subject, so great is its value, not only to the historian, biographer and genealogist, but also to the anthropologist, philologist, and even the collector of antiques! Would not the purchaser of the famous Pusey horn, with its "eleventh-century" inscription: "I King Knowde give William Pewse this horn to hold by thy lond" have hesitated before paying £1,800 had he been aware that surnames were unknown in Canute's day, even if he could not date the English used? Would not G. B. Shaw in *Saint Joan* have avoided his anachronism in naming a chaplain "John Bowyer Spencer Neville de Stogumber" had he known that in fifteenth-century England two names were rarely exceeded and four and five quite unknown? But, alas! a consideration of surnames is as yet the work of few outside the pedigree-maker and family historian.

Judging from the number of inquiries that I receive, many people are making investigation into the origin and meaning of their own designations, the birthright identifying them with their families. There being not fewer than 100,000 different surnames in use in the British Isles, the compilation of a volume giving evidence of the first form, and the signification of each appellative would be a monumental enterprise with a corresponding selling price, but pending the issue of such an encyclopædic work I hope that a short account illustrating the fundamental principles in name-composition will enable the new student to commence his research free from the commoner of the misunderstandings which have so beset the earlier inquirers into that department of etymology. The present epitome rests upon the system and doctrine of my compendious *History of Surnames of the British Isles* (1931), a heretical work if some critics are to be believed; thus a reviewer in the *Observer* (6 Sept., 1931), referring to my observation that comparatively few medieval nicknames have given rise to surnames, states that I "differ from all the European philologists who have handled the subject". I fear that the periodical has been misled on the point, but however that may be, few will deny that it is sometimes wise to revise opinions held from time immemorial, and examples of such ultimate enlightenment are constantly being exhibited in every branch of science. The length of time an historical error will remain current is remarkable, and nowhere is the perpetuation of absurdities more striking than in the realm of onomatology, so few early records being extant, and direct evidence consequently difficult to obtain. For instance, for over one hundred years nomenclaturists in succession have asserted that Anglo-Saxons occasionally bore hereditary surnames, the sole evidence consisting of a translation of a Cotton MS. originally presented by the eminent historian Sharon Turner (1799). In my above-cited book (pp. 59–62) I gave an amended reading of this document, which should end the propagation of that extraordinary delusion.

This undoubted proof that even an overwhelming majority is not always in the right will I hope add weight to my contention that not only curious and comical surnames, but also plain and apparently unmistakeable appellatives, are frequently anything but what they appear to be at sight, and therefore, no designation should be taken at face-value without strong proof. The more extensive my research becomes the more convinced I am of the correctness of this view, and while, in the present small volume, little evidence on any one point can be submitted, so important is this phase of name composition that I have devoted particular attention to an explanation of what may be termed the doctrine of synonymous change (see below, pp. 85-97). While this tenet will be held to be outrageous heterodoxy by those of the old school, who believe, for instance, that the epithet Nightingale was bestowed upon a vocalist of outstanding merit, I have little doubt that eventually the principle will become established as the common opinion.

The etymology of an appellative of unknown language is as difficult and uncertain as that of an archaic word severed from its context. With a place-name a clue may be obtained by surveying the site, if such be known, but with the surname evidence is difficult to obtain; for instance, I spent several months searching for examples of Shakespere, obtaining 250 examples for the 13th–15th centuries and even now, although the strong probability of several distinct origins appears, complete detailed information is wanting.

Some names make few appearances on the rolls, others fortunately can be traced much more easily, providing material for analysis, but the source of thousands yet remains obscure. The complete documentation includes the locality and date of origin, the language and the signification, and examples illustrating the various changes of form, and when the reference is to any one family, this data should be supported by genealogy, failing which any etymology can rank as little more than conjecture. It is generally fatal to accuracy to base any opinion on a single appearance, for instance, Bardsley saw in a printed record (Yorks. 1416) the curious name Mendfaute, which he thereupon put down as a complimentary sobriquet of one who busied himself repairing mistakes, but further examples would have shown the distinction to be that of a mendicant friar.

W. Mende*iu*ent, Yorks. 1266. (Ass. R. 1194, m.12.)
J. Mendfant, Westm. 1340. (G.D.135, m.13.)
W. Medfaunte, Yorks. 1379. (Poll Tax, VI, 131.)
J. Mendefant, Yorks. 1423. (K.B.29, 91, Mich. 2 Hen. 6.)
Thom. Johnson, mendyvaunt, Yorks. 1449. (K.B.9. 265, no. 22.)
Nich. Mendivaunt, Warw. 1475. (K.B.29, 113, 15 Edw. 4.)

It is clear that this northern description is neither Mend-fault, Mend-font, Mend-vent, nor any other nickname, and the examples are incidentally illustrative of the ever-recurring difficulty of distinguishing *u* from *n*. Happy-go-lucky etymology is by no means yet banished, a typical case from a modern book (Weekley, 1916, 133.) being "Mariota Gosebeck is a very evident nickname". This unfounded assertion would, however, not mislead the student, who remembers that *-beck* is a common element in place-names, and that at least one parish was called Gosbeck, even if he did not refer to the Hundred Rolls which read: "Dicunt quod Ric. *de* Gosebeck & Mariota ux' eius". Many of the popular nickname origins have no sounder foundation!

It being impossible within the limits of the present essay to find space for elaborating many names in the chronological manner, rather than the presentation of a series of unsupported derivations, efforts have been directed towards interesting the reader in the subject, providing an outline of the different formations, supplying examples for comparative study, and giving hints on the difficulties that may arise in tracing a name to its source. The possibility of discovering M.E. words unknown to dictionarians, will add to the pleasure of the study and the keenness of the searcher (see p. 156).

My examples are in most cases new, and to add to their value I have selected them largely from unpublished court records, in particular, choosing those where the names of the masses, the greatest preservers of O.E. appellatives, are most likely to be found, and I have made a special search for aliases, they often shedding most valuable light upon the subject.

In order that there may be no misunderstanding of my views I ask readers and critics to be so considerate as to read and digest the definitions of *surname* (p. 26), *description* (p. 26), and *nickname* (p. 166), and also to note, first, that no derivation should be considered final without obtaining the genealogy, or at least numerous dated instances for comparison, and secondly, that most names may be derived from two if not more distinct sources. This warning should be kept constantly in mind when studying the subject, as it is not practicable to print danger notices on every page. Having handled many thousands of ancient documents and rolls and scanned millions of medieval appellatives no person could be more convinced than I am of the uncertainty of the derivation of names of the British Isles.

C. L'ESTRANGE EWEN

103 Gower Street,
London, W.C.1.

CONTENTS

ABBREVIATIONS

Abb. Plac. Abbreviatio Placitorum.
Anc. D. Ancient Documents, P.R.O.
Ass. R. Assize Rolls.
Aug. Off. Augmentation Office, P.R.O.
Blk. Pr. Black Prince's.
Brit. British.
c. circa, about; century.
Cal. Calendar.
C5. Chancery Proceedings.
Cf. Compare.
Chanc. Chancery.
Chart. R. Charter Rolls.
Cl. R. Close Rolls.
Corn. Cornish.
Cor. R. Coroner's Roll.
Cott. Cotton.
C.P. P.R.O. reference for Common Pleas.
Ct. Court.
Cur. Reg. Curia Regis.
D.L. P.R.O. reference to Duchy of Lancaster records.
Doct. Document.
Dom. Bk. Domesday Book.
E. English.
E179. Class number for Subsidy Rolls.
E370. Exchequer L.T.R. Misc. Rolls.
e.g. for example.
E.H.S. *History of Surnames of the British Isles*, by C. L. Ewen, 1931.
Eng. English.
Exch. Exchequer.
f., *fem.* feminine.
For. Docts. Edited by J. H. Round.
Fr. French.
Gael. Gaelic.
G.D. Gaol Delivery Rolls.
gen. genitive.
Gr. Greek.
Hd. Hundred.
Heb. Hebrew.
Hund.R. Hundred Rolls.
Ibid. in the same place.
i.e. that is.
Inq. Inquisition.
Inq. Com. Cant. Inquisition Comitatus Cantabrigiensis.
Inq. p.m. Inquisitions post mortem.
Ir. Irish.
J. John.
Just. R. Justiciary Rolls.
K.B. P.R.O. reference for King's Bench.
Lat. Latin.
Lib. R. Liberate Rolls.
Lib. Wint. *Liber Wintoniensis.*

loc. local.
m. masculine, membrane.
M.E. Middle English.
MS. manuscript.
mod. modern.
N.E.D. *A New English Dictionary* (Murray).
N.F. Norman-French.
Norm. Norman.
obs. obsolete.
occ. occupational, occurs.
O.E. Old English.
O.F. Old French.
O.N. Old Norse.
or. In the examples represents *alias dictus* on the rolls.
Par. Parish.
Pard. R. Pardon Roll printed in *Letters and Papers*, For. and Dom. (Hen. VIII, 2nd. edit., vol. I, pp. 203-73).
Parl. R. Parliament Roll.
Pat. R. Patent Rolls.
Plac. de Q. W. Placita de quo Warranto.
P.R.O. Public Record Office.
R. Register, Roll.
Reg. Reginald.
Ric. Richard.
Rob. Robert.
Rot. de Obl. *Rotuli de Oblatis*, printed.
Salt. William Salt Arch. Soc.
Scand. Scandinavian.
S.C.2. Court Rolls, P.R.O.
St. Ch. Star Chamber.
Subs. Subsidy Roll, P.R.O. (E179).
Surt. Surtees.
Teut. Teutonic.
Thorpe. *Diplomatarium Anglicum*, 1865.
T.P. *Les Rôles de Taille Parisiens.*
W. Welsh, William.
Warw. Coll. R. Warwick College Rolls in P.R.O.
Wint. Winton.

CHAPTER I

THE RACES AND LANGUAGES OF BRITAIN AND IRELAND

The Races of Britain. Historians are commonly agreed that at the time of the Roman invasion (B.C. 55), the inhabitants of Britain were Iberians, Cymry, and Picts (of unknown origin), Ireland and the Isle of Man being populated by Gaels. Excepting the doubtful north of Scotland, the predominating tongues were Celtic, and doubtless the names also, since all being formerly descriptive words, they would tend to follow the spoken language. For about four centuries the Romans held sway over the Cymry, the speech being bilingual, Latin for the patricians and Celtic for the plebeians. The conquerors possessed a highly perfected method of nomenclature comprising prænomen (forename), nomen (clan name), cognomen (family name), with sometimes an agnomen derived from an illustrious deed, but with the fifth century and retiral of the legions, their heroic system passed, having taken no hold upon the fancy of the native Briton.[1]

No contemporary Celtic writings are extant, but it is to be inferred from later records that, in general, Cymry and Gaels were content with single names, which could be changed from time to time to appellatives thought to be more appropriate. So far as monumental inscriptions bear witness, the only secondary descriptions were those

[1] *E.H.S.*, pp. 44–7.

indicating parentage, such as in Eracobi maqi Eragetai, and Catgug f(il)ius Gideo, a method of naming which ultimately had great and permanent influence on the character of those of our surnames of Welsh, Scottish and Irish origin. The earliest Celtic chroniclers, who, it must be said, do not date back more than eight hundred years, gave their ancient kings and heroes more or less flattering additional epithets, placed after the personal names, as Enna Aighneach (*i.e.* complete was his hospitality), and some of these bygone heroes had a plurality of these descriptions, but their nature was individual and too transient to have any influence in moulding surnames.

Following upon the retiral of the Romans, the next change of importance was the advent of the Gothonic tribes, first as predatory bands, latterly as colonists, but success came tardily, and even by the end of the sixth century, after 150 years of intermittent fighting, the native Briton still ruled West Wales, *i.e.* Cornwall, Devon, and Somerset; North Wales, *i.e.* all territory west of the River Severn; and the great kingdom of Strathclyde extending from Buckinghamshire to the Clyde. The various Saxon tribes controlled all the eastern part of Britain, south of the River Forth, at first without unity among themselves, and not until the early ninth century did Ecgbert, king of the West Saxons, by subjugation of the other kingdoms, obtain the sole monarchy of Teutonic England. The Britons south of the River Dee likewise submitted to this monarch, the Picts, Scots, and Strathclyde Welsh alone remaining outside the confederation. Several centuries having elapsed since the first bodies of Teutons had established themselves in Britain, it is to be inferred that a good deal of intermarriage with the natives had taken place during that lengthy period, and it is, moreover, generally recognised that a large proportion of the inhabitants were entirely British in blood, language, and consequently names. Although the British tongue gradually gave way to English yet there are to-day about one million inhabitants who claim to speak Welsh.

Ireland remained purely Irish until, by the end of the eighth century, bodies of Northmen (Danes and Norwegians) effected settlements in that country. So successful became the adventurous Vikings that large territory in Northumbria and East Anglia also was ceded to them, and so harassed were Scotland and Strathclyde that they voluntarily submitted to Eadward (922–4), who thus became supreme head of all Britain. Danish invasions continuing with success, led up to Cnut, in 1017, becoming formally acknowledged king of Britain.

The Languages of Britain. This brief dip into history is necessary to show how the unknown languages of the aborigines must have yielded to Celtic tongues, which, except among the ruling classes during Roman occupation, flourished throughout all the British Islands, until they in turn gave way in large measure to the Ænglisc. Of great importance to the study of surnames is the possibility that in Strathclyde, the language of the Cymry lived until the fourteenth century,[1] and in Cornwall there were people, as late as the seventeenth century, who had little or no knowledge of the English language. In Brittany the ancient language and names survived, the latter being reintroduced to England at the Conquest, while in considerable parts of Wales, Man, Scotland, and Ireland, the Celtic tongues have been preserved to the present day. The Celtic languages

[1] Rev. J. Evans, *The Ancient Britons*, p. 103.

now to be heard in the British Isles are Irish, Gaelic (Scotland), Manx and Welsh. The Norse language, once current in the Viking settlements, may have been in use in certain districts in England down to the twelfth century,[1] and even to a later date in the Isle of Man, which, until 1219, remained under Scandinavian rule.

The Indo-European or Aryan languages are usually divided into six branches, (i) Indian; (ii) Iranian; (iii) Sarmatian; (iv) Celtic; (v) Græco-Latin; (vi) Gothic; the first three of which have had little effect upon the surnames of the British Isles. The Celtic branch (comprising Breton, Cornish, Welsh, Gaelic, Irish and Manx); the Græco-Latin branch (French, Walloon, Italian, etc.); and the Gothic branch comprising (i) the Teutonic subdivision (Anglo-Saxon or Old English, English, Scottish, Frisian, Dutch, Flemish and German), and (ii) the Scandinavian subdivision (Icelandic, Norwegian, Danish, etc.), all combined in the making of our surnames.[2] An axiomatic principle to be absorbed is that race, language, and personal names do not depend upon one another, and are often found to differ in one nation.

The Personal Names of Britain. A realisation of the number of languages spoken in Britain will introduce the perplexities to be faced in determining the origin of any name, a difficulty much greater than that to be overcome by the etymologist who determines the ancient form and signification of a word, such being usually contextually placed.

Our names at the time of the Norman Conquest (1066) were mainly Anglo-Saxon (Old English), Cornish, Welsh, Manx, Scandinavian, Gaelic, (Scottish), with

[1] E. Ekwall, *Intro. to English Place-names*, vol. I, pt. i, p. 92.
[2] *E.H.S.*, p. 22.

Irish, generally throughout Ireland; but with the coming of Duke William, another great change swept over Britain. Just as the native names, Gethin, Ithel, Griffith, Angharad, and so on, had given way to the Beorhtric, Leofwine, Ulfketel and Ealdgyth of the Gothic tribes, so did the latter yield in turn to the Roger, Hamo, John and Matilda of the new-comers. Nevertheless considerable numbers of the interesting Old English appellatives maintained their popularity, mainly among the lower orders, ultimately to become established as family names gracing the modern directories. The names of the followers of William of Normandy were mainly French, often of Teutonic origin, as his own (Wilhelm), but one-third of his supporters at the decisive battle of Hastings being Bretons, a re-introduction of Celtic names also occurred.

Commercial intercourse with the Continent having been opened up, the never-ending flow of aliens commenced, Flemings, Frisians, Lombards, Dutchmen, Spaniards, Hebrews and other enterprising foreigners making Britain their happy hunting ground and final resting place. At first identified by single names, in the twelfth century they commenced to introduce surnames, although those of striking foreign sound were soon abandoned or moulded into a shape more palatable to the English tongue, the final forms, as now found in the directories, providing the investigator with some of the most interesting problems in the realm of etymology.

Classification of Personal Names. Since about one-third of British surnames are derived from personal appellatives, it is of interest to give some attention to their composition. Names of the Indo-European group can be arranged conveniently, according to form and construction, in three main classes.

1. *Dithematic or Compounded.* This class consists of names compounded of two themes or components, which members or elements have been termed appropriately, the prototheme and deuterotheme respectively.[1] Such appellatives are sometimes called "full-names" as opposed to "short-names", being those having but one theme.

The elements may be (i) two nouns, as Faol-chadh, Ir. 'wolf-warrior'; Cad-waladyr, W. 'war-chief' (*cad*, 'battle': *gwaladr*); Ceol-mund, O.E. 'ship-protection'; (ii) a noun preceded by a qualifying adjective, as Fionn-bharr, Ir. 'fair-head'; Gryf-fydd (W. *cref*, 'strong'; *fydd*, 'faith'); Dun-stan, O.E. 'brown-rock'; or followed by the adjective, as Bairr-fhionn, Ir., Pen-wyn, W. 'fair-head'; Here-berht, O.E. 'bright army'. In Irish compounds more complicated formations may be found, as Dubh-dá-inbhear, 'black of the two river mouths'.

While anciently the words chosen for the construction of names had in conjunction, some sensible meaning descriptive of the bearer, even if figuratively and prophetically, in later days the combination of two vocables, with a total disregard of the resulting significance, was practised.[2] A full appreciation of the extent of such name-building among the Anglo-Saxons is of immense importance to the subject, because, although many actual examples of O.E. appellatives cannot now be obtained, yet, from a knowledge of the elements, a name can often be reconstructed, thus, if we know of Beorhtsige and Leofric, it is a fair inference that Sigebeorht, Sigeleof, Sigeric, Beorhtleof, Beorhtric, Leofbeorht, Leofsige, Ricbeorht, Ricsige and Ricleof were

[1] *E.H.S.*, p. 25.

[2] For fuller details of Irish names see P. Woulfe; for O.E., the works of J. M, Kemble, S. Turner, W. G. Searle, and M. Redin. For early Gothonic names. *E.H.S.*, chap iii, and for Welsh names, *E.H.S.*, pp. 39–43, 121–7.

also names at one time. Actually, nearly all such designations are to be traced, but the principle is equally sound with unrecorded designations, and these it may be assumed far outnumber those preserved in extant documents. It may be noted that a neuter noun cannot supply the final element, and the deuterotheme is usually of the same gender as the person upon whom the name was bestowed.[1]

2. *Monothematic or Uncompounded.* In this class appear names having a single original element, and also, since they are indistinguishable, diminished forms of dithematic names. Monothematic names may be exemplified by an adjective, as Breac, Ir. 'speckled'; or a noun, as Budic, W. (*buddug*, f. 'the victorious one'). The Anglo-Saxons had many single-element names, such as Beorn, Dudda, Hune, Lulle, etc., but these were probably originally components of dithematic names.

3. *Derivatives.* Into this category are placed names derived from those of (1) and (2) by various processes, such as prefixion, suffixion, subtraction of letters and syllables, or changes in form. Among such derivatives are hypocorisms (pet-names), diminutives, and augmentatives, but their identification is often uncertain.

The suffixes are of the greatest importance, and the tendency being to shorten compound names before adding the termination, a variety was introduced which greatly multiplied the genealogical surnames of the British Isles. Suffixes having diminutive force were popular with the Irish, as Dubh, Dubhán, Duibhín, Dubhagán, and to a lesser extent with the Welsh, as Bleddyn, 'a wolf's cub' (*blaidd*, 'a wolf'). In Irish surnames the influence of diminutives is evidenced by the

[1] For example of name-building, *E.H.S.*, p. 52, and the lists of elements pp. 366–72.

large number ending in *n*. The O.E. suffixes will be noticed in a further section (p. 62).

Additional Descriptions. The ancient chronicles identify persons by either single or double designations, in the latter case the first distinctions being the font-names, the second, in general, fanciful epithets, in most instances, it may be surmised, bestowed posthumously. These secondary labels, secondary both in position and value, are worthy of notice because later on they tended to repeat themselves in the same family, and finally became fixed as surnames, and of first importance. Such distinctions are classifiable under four heads which may be termed (i) Characteristic, answering the question—What is his personal peculiarity? (ii) Local, answering—Where is or was he located? (iii) Genealogical, answering—Who is his most important kinsman? (iv) Occupational, answering—What is his vocation? The following examples of pre-Norman period are instructive:—

Characteristic. These descriptions may relate to the bearer's appearance, as Enna Derg (Ir. 'the red'); Rys Voel (W. 'the bald'); Wulfric se Blaca (O.E. 'the black'); Ægelsig the reáda (O.E. 'the red'); Thurkil Hwitá (O.E. 'the white'); Æilwine yunge; Lifolfr Skalli (N. 'bald pate'); or to character, as Cormac Cas (Ir. 'the cruel'); Howel Da (W. 'the good'); Thurcyl Hoga (O.E. 'the wise'); Hakon Galinn (N. 'the silly'). Physical attributes might be perpetuated, as Conall Guthbind (Ir. 'sweet-voiced'); Benlli Gawr (*cawr*, W. 'giant'); or possessions might be noted, as Oenghus Ollmuccaid (*ollmucca*, Ir. 'great swine'); Osla Gyllelvawr (W. 'the great knife'). Some second names described acts of the bearer, or events which occurred during his life, as Aed Gusdan (*gus*, Ir. 'deed'; *dana*, Ir. 'bold'); Eochu Apthach (Ir.

'the deadly', from the pestilence prevalent in his time). The condition or quality of a person also gave rise to epithets, as Sirna Saeglach (Ir. 'long-lived'); Helen Luiedauc (W. 'the prosperous') ; Ælfsige Cild (O.E. 'the child'). Strangers might be dubbed with their nationality, as Rein Yscot (W. 'the Scot'); Ælfword Kæntisce. Metaphorical and fanciful descriptions were common with the Celts, as Chynan Genhir (*gên*, W. 'life'; *hir*, 'long').

Local. Descriptions from place-names occur rarely in Celtic narratives, as, Cairbre Luachra (Ir. 'of Luachair'); Tutuwlch Cornue (W. 'of Cornwall'). The Old English examples take different forms according to the language of the record:—(i) c. 1018, Leofwine æt Hortune. (ii) c. 962, Ælfgar on Meapaham. (iii) c. 962, Godwin de Fecham. (iv) c. 1050, Osgod apud Heailea. (v) c. 1060, Ælfwin Gortune.

Genealogical. Description by reference to the most important kinsman was common with Celtic races, as for example, Conmael mac Emir (*mac*, Ir. 'son'); Cormac ua Cuind, *i.e.* grandson of Conn. *Ua* became *O*, and has had a great influence in the formation of Irish surnames, of which so many commence with O', but the popular prefix never became known in the Isle of Man. In Welsh, *map* is equivalent to the Irish *mac*, both formerly being *maqv-i*, and is found as *vap*, *mab*, *fab*, etc., and later still as *ap* and *ab*. Words specifying the filial relationship were frequently latinised, as Catteli *filius* Brohcmail. Four systems of O.E. genealogical descriptions have been noticed:—(i) 547, Benoc [wæs] Branding. (ii) *ante* 1056, Godwine Earwiges sunu. (iii) 962, Wulfeg filius Ordegi. (iv) 1033, Godwine Brytæl.

Occupational. Description by vocation is rare in

early Celtic records, but became commoner with the Anglo-Saxons. Some examples are: Irél Faith (Ir. 'the prophet'); Ælfere ealdorman.

The Suffix-ing. Surnames are often found with the termination *-ing*, but owing to several applications it is not always possible, at sight, to determine its exact signification. Formerly it functioned in lieu of a filial desinence, as in Eoppa Esing, where it seems to have a prepositional force equal to 'of', and implying 'son of', as in the colloquial expression, Will o' Dick's. It also had the broader sense equivalent to Ir. *ua*, 'descendant of'; and again in surnames derived from place-names may signify 'meadow'. *Ing* also occurs as an element in personal names as Ingwulf, and the diminished form has become perpetuated in the well-known surname Inge.[1]

Description and Surname. The word 'surname' has been of wide application, and some writers yet employ it to signify any secondary appellative bestowed upon an individual. Such usage leads to considerable confusion, and in the present essay the individual distinction is termed a 'description' until its application becomes extended to all members of the family, when it ranks as a surname. The nature of the surname has been more particularly expressed as follows:—

"The additional epithets or descriptions concurrently developed into hereditary names of two different types. One such type is a patronymic inherited or perpetuated only by the eldest legitimate sons in succession; the second type is the family name, as we have it to-day, a patronymic of a male parent, the common right of user being inherited at birth by all legitimate children of the bearer, the sons only of whom transmit it to their legitimate children, and so on, generation after generation. By the nomenclaturist, the word 'inheritance' is used in the sense of a birthright, which passes at birth, and independently of the death of the parent, and is a right to joint

[1] *E.H.S.*, pp. 57–9.

user, but not a right to sole ownership. In English law there is no property in a surname."[1]

Great antiquity is claimed for family names by the Chinese,[2] and in Japan a record of surnames was published as early as A.D. 815,[3] but in Europe, search as we like, no adoption of hereditary designations at so remote a date can be traced. The Anglo-Saxons had no family names, and were usually content with single appellatives, sometimes a theme of which might be repeated in those of the children, thus Æthelstan and Wulfgifu might baptise son and daughter, Wulfstan and Æthelgifu respectively. Saxon pedigrees show that adoption of one initial was also practised; for instance, of thirty descendants of Ecgbryht, twenty-nine had names commencing with Æ, E or Ea; and of Sledda's posterity nineteen out of twenty had the initial S. In Wales, as is well known, the native method of identifying a person was to recite his genealogy backwards for half a dozen generations or so, and that pedigree system of distinction continued for long after hereditary family names had become general throughout the British Isles.

In the Lowlands of Scotland a practice in parallel with that of England, became customary, but the highlanders continued the genealogical system of Ireland. Some writers assign the first Irish surnames to the tenth century, but direct evidence on the point is entirely wanting, and moreover, the twelfth-century *Cóir Anmann* which gives the significations of a number of secondary descriptions, contains no indication whatsoever of their hereditary nature, and it seems that only

[1] *E.H.S.*, pp. 73–4.
[2] *China Review*, XIII (1884–5), p. 124.
[3] T. Harada.

English influence caused such a system to come into being.

Although the custom of Gaels, Cymry, Saxons and Northmen, in using for distinction, secondary descriptions or addresses in addition to their forenames provided all the necessary material for making surnames, yet before the coming of William the Conqueror hereditary family appellatives were unknown in the British Isles.

CHAPTER II

THE INTRODUCTION AND DEVELOPMENT OF SURNAMES

The Norman Conquest, A.D. 1066. The defeat of Harold at the battle of Hastings by the combined forces of Normans, Bretons, and Frenchmen, under the command of William, duke of Normandy, led to another great change in the personal names of the British Isles. In the eleventh century, the language of the Normans, commonly called Norman-French, was a debased Latin, embracing Teutonic, Celtic, and Scandinavian elements, and their personal names had similar characteristics, the formation, therefore, following that already outlined. A feature having great influence in multiplying variants of our names was the number of diminutive suffixes introduced in later years. Notwithstanding that French became the language of the upper classes, law courts, and schools, English remained the spoken tongue of the people, ultimately to supersede all others. Any chance that the Celtic names of Brittany had of becoming established received a severe check by the failure of the revolt of Ralph de Guader in 1075.

Examination of early Continental records points to the Normans being about as far advanced in the use of second names as the English, and their descriptions fall into the same four classes.

Feudal System. An innovation of Norman creation was the organisation of crown feoffees, who held land by vassalage, in return for services, usually military. Under this system the tenant in chief naturally became known by the name of his fief, "the foundation of his value to his suzerain, and measure of his importance in the world".[1] The same distinction, being applied in time to the eldest son and his successors, came by constant repetition to be looked upon as the description of the family, ultimately crystallising into the hereditary surname. Similar names were often acquired by serviles, and numbers of Englishmen bear designations corresponding to Norman fiefs, such as Vere, Daubeney, etc., without being descendants of those first known by the names, or ever owning any land.

Domesday Book, the historic territorial survey of the English lands of the Conqueror, completed in 1086, notices thousands of persons, but owing to the official scribe's praiseworthy attempts to economise parchment, many second-names were omitted, they being considered of very little importance in those days. Of the personal names large numbers are Saxon and Norman, with a sprinkling of Cymric, as Griffin, Rees; Gaelic, as Ghilander (servant of Andrew); Meurdoch (now Murdoch); Scandinavian, as Chetel (now Kettle), Strang; Flemish, as Lanbert, Drogo; and Hebrew, as Adam and Isac. Many of the personal names afterwards became established as family names.

Descriptions of the Norman Period, A.D. 1086-1154. In records of the eleventh and twelfth centuries appellatives, both personal and secondary, are very frequently latinised, often with confusing results, as evidenced below (p. 89). A plenitude of examples, English and Latin (French influence being slight), may be found in the various Domesday Books, *Liber Wintoniensis*, etc., often in very corrupt form.

[1] *E.H.S.*, p. 80.

Characteristic descriptions. In this section are epithets relating to personal appearance, as Robertus Niger (the black), Alestan Hwit (the white), Aluric Parvus (the small), Aluric Petit (the small); or to character, as Edric Salvage (the ferocious). Other descriptions relate to condition or quality, as Ricardus Juvenis (the young), Edricus Cecus (the blind); or to race, as Tehelus Britto, Godwin Francigena, and Strang Danus.

Local descriptions. English *æt* and *on* having fallen into disuse, distinctions in this class are of three types. (i) Robert de Verli, Alured de Ispania, Bruman de laforda. (ii) Alured Hispaniensis (of Spain); Hugo Flandriæ (of Flanders); Hugo Silvestris (of the wood). The *-ensis* type fell into disuse after the middle of the twelfth century. (iii) Hugo Bolebec. Possibly also Edric Chuet and Alwin Poplestan.

Genealogical descriptions. Three types are to be noted. (i) Norman Merewine sune, Leuric Hobbesune, Godric Chingessone. (ii) Hugo filius Grip, Godwin filius Toka, Griffin filius Mariadoc. (iii) Eduin Alferd, Hubert Flohard. The *-ing* form of genealogical termination had ceased to be used, and for two hundred years the filial desinence *-son* suffered an eclipse.[1]

Occupational descriptions. Additions of vocation were commonly in Latin, as Theodric coquus, Goscelinus loremarius (the bit-maker, now Lorimer), rarely in English, as Godwin Dancere.

An analysis of several thousand names shows that by the end of the Norman period 83 per cent of persons were given secondary descriptions in the official rolls.[2]

Descriptions of the Plantagenet Period, A.D. 1154-1485. The records covering the first two cen-

[1] *E.H.S.*, pp. 102, 172.
[2] *E.H.S.*, p. 100.

turies of the Angevin or Plantagenet dynasty are perhaps the most interesting to the student of English surnames. We see Latin names ousted by French, that in turn give way to English, and we obtain the earliest contemporary examples of Welsh, Cornish, Scottish, Manx, and Irish names, and learn in what manner and to what degree they were influenced by English. The gradual growth of the hereditary nature of the descriptions is evidenced. Of immense importance to the subject are (i) the arrival of swarms of aliens from the Low Countries, France, Italy, Germany, Denmark, Spain, etc., and (ii) the spread of the Celtic element, southward from Scotland, eastward from Ireland, in every direction from Wales, and Cornwall, and northward from Brittany.[1] Elements of great interest too are the rise and decline in the use of Scandinavian and Hebrew appellatives. The lists of names become plentiful, Exchequer rolls and records of the King's Court, commencing in the twelfth century, and running on in unbroken series, providing a wealth of material of most absorbing variety.

Norman Personal Names. Baptismal names have had such a great influence in the making of British surnames that careful analysis to ascertain the relative prevalence of O.E. and Norman font-names has been made. Taking the Pipe Roll for the year 1130–1 (64 years after the Conquest) it was found that already the interesting O.E. names had almost ceased to be used, nearly 90 per cent being Norman or biblical, [2] but it has to be noted that, in general, these records do not provide many good lists of the designations of the lower orders. A count from the Rotuli Curiæ Regis for the year 1200 gave 93 per cent, and from the Hundred Rolls, 1275,

[1] Ewen, *Are the British "Anglo-Saxons" or Celts?* 1938,
[2] *E.H.S.*, p. 99.

99 per cent, investigation in this latter case being confined to the servile classes, where the Saxon names were most likely to have been preserved.[1] Of the 93 per cent alien names in 1200, William, the most popular, accounted for 14 per cent, Richard 9 per cent, Robert 8 per cent, Ralph 6 per cent, Roger, Walter, John, and Thomas, 5 per cent each, Henry 3 per cent, Geoffrey, Gilbert, Hugh, Reynold, and Simon, 2 per cent each, the remaining 23 per cent of alien entries covering sixty-nine different appellatives.[2] All these names are, of course, given in the rolls in the Latin form, which, except for the termination, rarely differs from the English. By 1275 (among the lower orders) William had increased to 19 per cent, being followed by John, 16 per cent, Richard, 10 per cent, and Robert, 7 per cent, the remaining 47 per cent being made up by twenty-eight different names. It is evident that a very small variety of personal designations was in use, and only one per cent English. Fortunately these figures are not absolutely representative, and considerably more O.E. names survived, as will be evidenced in another manner.

Survival of English Names. Although native personal appellatives make such a small exhibit in these records, it is satisfactory to find many preserved as second-names, and well on the way to becoming surnames. Taking again the Rotuli Curiæ Regis for 1200, of secondary descriptions of the genealogical class, no fewer than 36 per cent were found to be Old English. Among servile tenants in 1275, O.E. secondary descriptions outnumbered O.E. personal names by ten to one. These secondary descriptions not being preceded by

[1] *E.H.S.*, pp. 109, 120.
[2] *E.H.S.*, pp. 120, 188.

filius have the appearance of being settled surnames or well on the way to becoming so. It cannot, however, be claimed that they had become so established before the decline in the use of Saxon font-names had set in, few hereditary names being then known, and "three possible reasons for the apparent multiplication present themselves:—(i) the more characteristic nature of the O.E. names may have tended to their preservation as distinctive additions in greater proportion than the Norman; appellatives such as William and John being of comparatively small service for the purpose, the bearers of Norman names would be the most likely to acquire descriptions of other classes. (ii) Teutonic names after losing popularity in this country may have been reintroduced by aliens; but unfortunately no means exist of determining to what extent. (iii) In some parts of the country O.E. designations may have been much better preserved than generally appears; an excellent example of such survival being a list of names of men of Lynn (Norf.) in 13 Hen. II (1166–7), to be found on the Pipe Rolls."[1] So interesting and exceptional are these appellatives that a selection follows:—

Blacheman, Brixi, Godard, Godebald, Gouti, Hunger, Ketelbern, Leuiet, Richolf, Sparche, Staingrim, Suift, Sunnulf.

Godw' fil' Ædilde, Turoldus fil' Ælueue, Tomas fil' Ailmeri, Alfward fil' Alfware, Aluricus fil' Alsued', Ædwinus Attebal, Aluricus Attewas, Turstinus Barill, Hadebrand fil' Biffe, Ric' Chelloc, Will's Chide, Rob' Cholle, Godw' Crec, Sum'da Cusin, Algar fil' Elnod, Turold Flobi, Staingrim fil' Gamel, Ric' fil' Geue, Rob' fil' Gliuman, Hugo fil' Gochi, Walt' Godcheap, Gamel fil' Godr', Brihtmer fil' Hereward, Aluric Hocheweder, Wulm' Horn, Godw' Horngrai, Bo'de Hund, Radbode fil' Ilhuge, Seman joculator, Sibald Kiker, Ric' fil' Leftred', Wulnod' Lellesmai, Hagene Locheburs, Godebald Lurc, Godman fil' Munne, Strangrim nouus, Turchetil fil' Oggi, Siricius

[1] *E.H.S.*, p. 121.

fil' Osfrid', Suetman Parmenter, Anscetil parvus, Ric' Pilecat, Erneis Pine, Ric' Rotefot, Sim' Sittebid'cunte, Rob' Struntard, Wulnoth fil' Suartgari, Rad' fil' Tette, Rob' fil' Theini, Godw' fil' Titte, Wrange Toch', Ædward fr' Turoldi, Godlamb de Well', Godman Wid'er (Wicher), Hugo Wisman, Will's fil' Wulsi.[1]

The main list consists of 138 persons, of whom 39 have double and 17 single O.E. or Norse names, 31 others having O.E. baptismal names with Latin, local or other descriptions. In 24 cases, sons of Englishmen have Norman personal names, only 27 persons exhibiting no English influence whatsoever.

This wealth of O.E. names is very much in excess of that found elsewhere at this early period, for instance, a glance at the coeval *Liber Niger Scaccarii*, a list of names of the upper classes, shows practically none of O.E. origin. Here, on the Pipe Roll on the contrary, are interesting examples of Blackman, Goodlamb, and Swift, as font-names, and a step further has been reached with Barrell, Kellock, Kidd, Creake, Cousin, Gammell, Geves, Goodchap, Horn, Munn, Pyne, Tate, Thain, Tuck, Wiseman, and others, which as second-names, are on the way to becoming surnames. The majority of the second-names have been baptismal, but Crec may be Creake (15 miles from Lynn). Blackman, Goodlamb, and Swift, erroneously classed by Bardsley and others, as nicknames, disclose their true nature, and it may be realised from this valuable illustration, that many curious names, hitherto taken at face-value and given a modern signification, are much more likely to be survivals of Anglo-Saxon personal names with an entirely different meaning, *e.g.* Lemon, Rainbow, Reindeer, Snowball, Turbot, Vinegar, Whisker, etc., are most improbably ridiculous epithets as commonly

[1] Pipe Roll, 1166–7, pp. 20–9.

supposed, but rather good old English names of great antiquity.

Plurality of Descriptions. Of so little permanent value were the secondary descriptions in the twelfth century that, on the one hand, numbers of persons from the King downwards had nothing of the kind, and on the other hand, some commoners boasted distinction by several different designations. No better example can be given than that first noticed by Camden in the Visitation of Cheshire (1580). William Belward of Malpas (Ches.) had two sons David (de Malpas) and Richard; David had three sons, variously distinguished in the Latin genealogy as de Malpas, Gough, and de Golborne; Richard's five sons were known as de Cotgreve, de Overton, Litell, de Hampton, and de Coddington; Gough had a son described as Egerton, and a grandson Wigland; Golborne's second son was pedigreed as de Goodman; Little had a son Kenen le Clerk, and a son of Hampton was called Houa Bras. No dates are given, but the family evidently flourished in the thirteenth century. Here may be seen in the one family, characteristic, local, and occupational descriptions with every chance of resulting ultimately in fourteen different surnames; and a bearer of any one might himself be known by two or more distinctions. For instance, Richard son of Gilbert Crispin does not occur as Richard Crispin in the Domesday Survey, 1086, but as Ricardus filius Gisleberti (Kent, 14), and Ricardus de Tonebridge (*ibid.*); moreover, Ordericus Vitalis (1073) names him Ricardus de Benefacta (*i.e.* de Bienfaite), and elsewhere he is called Ricardus de Clare.[1]

Comparative Features, A.D. 1327. The recording clerks, by the end of the twelfth century, considered it a

[1] *E.H.S.*, p. 110

duty to give every person a mark of identification, and it is rare to find thereafter any person without an official secondary description, but such indicia were by no means uniform in character throughout the country. An excellent means of comparing the peculiarities exists in the Exchequer Subsidy Rolls for the year 1327, one of the few sets to escape the results of the neglect of the custodians of past centuries. In the North the great use of *filius* and *de* demonstrates that few persons had 'to-names', the scribe having to make shift with name of parent or address, and an analysis of Lancashire appellatives showed that only six per cent of persons were labelled with descriptions that could rank as surnames, and even at the present day among the villagers, little use is made of second names. In Lancashire, as in counties bordering on Wales, the extensive use of *filius* was due to the late retention of the old Cymric system of genealogical distinction. In the southern parts of England such employment had almost entirely ceased. In the South also, the preposition *de* was much less used than in the North, being largely replaced by English prepositions. A special feature of northern names was the growth in the employment of the desinence 'son'. The descriptions of Cornwall stand out distinctly owing to the number of addresses, but prepositions in their composition were sparingly used, and then nearly always in Latin. The article *le* in the formation of characteristic and occupational descriptions, almost unknown in the most northern counties and Lincolnshire, was fairly uniform practice elsewhere, with the exception of Kent.[1]

Secondary descriptions without filial expression, preposition, or article, the immediate forerunners of sur-

[1] The student may refer to statistical table, *E.H.S.*, p. 170.

names, were becoming increasingly common, but much more so in the South than in the North. An analysis of several thousands of names gave the figures 39 per cent for Cumberland, 52 to 70 per cent for the Midland Counties, and 83 per cent for Cornwall, the latter being exceptional figures and largely addresses.[1] Names not readily classifiable tend to increase, due no doubt to the presence of many foreign appellatives in corrupt form. In the north of England it may be estimated that not more than 6 per cent of the people were known by hereditary family names, the average for the whole country being about 50 to 60 per cent.

Prepositional Descriptions. In addition to *de*, other Latin prepositions were in use, such as *ad*, *in*, *super*, and *juxta*, but they are more frequently to be found in records of the central counties than in those of the north. In the Pipe Rolls for the year 1230, English prepositions, after a long rest, commence to make a few appearances, such as de Atteholm, de Boveton, Bovewode, and it is evident that they have only passed the clerk through a misunderstanding arising from coalescence. In the South, less Latin and more English is evidenced in the fourteenth century, such descriptions being found, as Binetheton, Bysowthewimpel, Hunderewalle, Onyemyre (bog), Othemarsh, Sidernefenne, Underthebrygg, Wythouthetown, etc. The preposition in commonest use was *at*, as atter lake, atte clougres (*clowre*, 'turf'), ate pette (pit), atten elmes (modern Nelmes), etc. The interchangeability of Latin, French, and English is illustrated by, de Broke, de la Broke, and Attebroc; ad Portam (gate), de la Zate (z=yogh), ate Yate.

By the sixteenth century, except for the cases of

[1] *E.H.S.*, p. 171.

coalescence, as in Bywater, Underwood, etc., the preposition had entirely died out, but it had been the means of establishing almost every known object of hill and dale as an hereditary family appellative. In this manner we obtained such surnames, as Apps (O.E. *æsp*, 'the aspen'), Clive (steep side of a hill), Knapp (summit of a hill), Shute (Corn. 'watering place'), Snappe (a spring), Slade (a dell), Worth (an enclosed place), and so on. Late examples are:

Thom. a Keys, Leic. 1523. (Subs. E179, 133/108.)
Step. a Talys, Leic. 1523. (Subs. E179, 133/108.)

Cornish treatment of the preposition *ate* is worth notice:

Edita ata ville, 1327. (Subs. E179, 87/7, m.16.)
Thom. ata Lane, 1327. (Subs. E179, 87/7, m.16.)

Inheritance of Descriptions. As early as 1267, a verdict of a London jury evidences that it had come to be understood that a man's "true name" was that borne by his father,[1] but centuries elapsed before the custom became generally recognised, and even now the law does not insist upon such repetition. It may be asked—How can it be known when a description has become a surname? Provided a pedigree is available, the determination of the stage of permanence reached by the name presents no difficulty, but without the genealogy for reference any opinion can be nothing more than surmise.

Characteristic descriptions. If a person, who by custom has been dubbed with a name denoting his appearance, character, relationship, nationality, or other attribute,

[1] *Cal. of Inq. Misc.* (*Chanc.*), vol. I, p. 183; *E.H.S.*, p. 383.

has one or more children not possessing such attribute, but who are likewise designated, the second name has become an inherited surname.

Local descriptions. In the case where a tenant who has been distinguished by the name of his land is succeeded by son or grandson similarly named, it does not follow that the name has become a perpetual inheritance of that family. Loss or disposal of those lands might quite easily result in a new name being adopted. If, on the other hand, the name were taken by members of the family born after such loss or disposal, then it might reasonably be looked upon as an hereditary surname.

Genealogical descriptions. If Robert had a son called William, who was described as William Robert's son, and if William's son became likewise distinguished as Robertson instead of Williamson, it is clear that Robertson had acquired all the characteristics of the modern surname.

Occupational descriptions. In similar manner, if William, son of John the cook, became known as William Cook, although he followed a different vocation from that of his father, it is a fair inference that Cook had become the hereditary surname of that family.[1]

An analysis of descriptions on the Poll Tax Rolls, 1377, showed that 24 per cent employed *filius*, *de*, *le*, *atte*, etc., leading to the conclusion that not more than 76 per cent of persons could have had hereditary second-names. In the South the proportion was greater, but in the North, particularly in Lancashire, surnames were rarely used. Many appellatives which from appearance alone might reasonably be classed as hereditary surnames may, by chance, be discovered to be otherwise.

[1] *E.H.S.*, p. 187.

Ric. Godman, pat' Osberti Bron, Warw. 1262. (Ass. R. 954, m. 10d.)

Geof. Wodeman fil' Joh'ne Sclaulewik, Hants, 1334. (G.D. 120, m. 8.)

Alan de Penruddok, fil' Joh'ne Henrison, Cumb. 1382. (Anc. D. C3975.)

Greg. Couper fil' Henr' Barbour, Warw. 1435. (K.B.9, 227, no. 87.)

The number of aliases on 15th cent. rolls also demonstrates the unsettled nature of surnames:—Elisius Tomesson alias dictus Elesius Johnson, Norf., 1474 (G.D. 209, m. 13).

Manifold Names and Descriptions. As stated above, by the end of the thirteenth century, the clerk rarely entered a name on an official roll without an accompanying description or address. Occasionally in the tenth and eleventh centuries, double distinctions, such as a characteristic description and an address, had been used, and examples are found sparingly in succeeding centuries. In the case of Roger Paye Levedey, Yorks. (Cl. R., 1288), probably nothing more is meant than Roger son of Paye Levedey. In the fourteenth century, double surnames were produced in the North through the prevalent custom of combining *son* with the patronymic such as John Dicson Robynson, that is John the son of Dick the son of Robin. More complicated descriptions are to be found:—

"Rog'us le Vertere Adamesman le cotiller de Trompeton" (Beds. 1315; G.D.1, m. 12).

That is, Roger the verter, the man of Adam the cutler. Verter is not known to dictionarians, but is otherwise the verderer.

In Cornwall it became the recognised practice to combine the son's personal name with the father's two names, as William Jakke Jowy, and more rarely with three paternal appellatives, as Hugo Richard Jak Felyp,[1] indicating, it is to be supposed, unless two names have run together, that Hugh was son of Richard, son of Jack Philip. Another Cornish peculiarity is that two names of the parent were commonly combined, as Roger Hikharry, Thomas Jakhencock. (1437.)[2]

In Welsh records may be found treble or quadruple names due, in like manner, to the omission of *ap*, or perhaps to the addition of a nickname, *e.g.* Thomas Morgan Thlewellyn Thee, Heref. 1485,[3] and so in Scotland and Ireland, patronymic, clan-name, and nickname were strung together quite in the style of the Romans, as Thadeus oge (the young) McTeige O'Harte, and in a case like Patrick Fitz George og of Galway, merchant, 1603, there are four descriptions, genealogical, characteristic, local, and occupational.

Examination of parish registers shows that few double christian names were given until the eighteenth century, but in recent years three and four have become not uncommon, and in the case of one unfortunate infant no fewer than twenty-six were bestowed at the font. In the nineteenth century, double, treble, quadruple and even quintuple surnames joined by hyphens came into fashion, forming most cumbersome family names.[4] An early hyphenated example is found in a record of 1635: De Rogero Harrie=Yonge (Cl. R. Index, 10 Chas., 8 pt. 15).

[1] K.B. 29, 113, Hil. 18 Edw. 4.
[2] K.B. 9, 233, no. 83.
[3] K.B. 29, 116, m. 11.
[4] As Temple-Nugent-Brydges-Chandos-Grenville.

CHAPTER III

THE POLYGLOT NATURE OF BRITISH SURNAMES

Influence of Aliens. A study of the greatest importance is the effect of the constant flow of foreigners into Britain. Down till the year 1558 England had Continental possessions, and a steady cross-Channel traffic being maintained, not only Bretons, Normans, Angevins, Burgundians, Poitevins, Champenois, etc., from various parts of France, but Brabanters and Flemings from the Low Countries, Florentines and Lombards from Italy, Spaniards and Germans, with a plentiful quota of Jews (*ante* 1290), established themselves in Britain. Few of the strangers can have retained their native names in the original orthographic form, and the more popular the English language became the less did the clerks attempt to preserve the alien spelling and signification, but twisted the foreign appellative into something with an English sound. In this way numbers of curious names were created, some examples of which will be found below. The alien designation might also be dropped entirely and replaced by (i) the country of origin or race, as Champagne, Brabazon, etc., (ii) a new English descriptive name, as Newman, Carpenter, Hawthorne, or (iii) a translation, as White for Weiss or Blanche.[1]

French Descriptions. One hundred years passed

[1] *E.H.S.*, p. 134.

after the Conquest before the legal authorities deigned to accept French words as secondary descriptions in any appreciable quantity. The Pipe Roll of A.D. 1174–5 provides a number of examples, as Odo 'de la Faleisia', Petrus 'Petit grant', other entries again being a combination of Latin, French and English, as Alanus le Neucument. By the year 1230 French had become common usage, such names appearing as Barbe de Or (gold beard); le Bel (the handsome; now Bell); le Buffle (the fool or jester); le Goyz (the lame; now possibly Goose); la Papa (the priest, father; now Pope); and le Sage (the wise; now Sage).

The Article.[1] In Latin there is no article, but the demonstrative pronoun *ille*, 'that,' reduced to two cases, became in O.F. *li* (subjective case) and *le* (objective case), the feminine form being *la*. The subjective case becoming obsolete, left the modern French *le*, *la*, *les*. Although names were formerly latinised, in the first half of the twelfth century the scribes began to use the article *le* in the composition of descriptions, as exemplified above, but by the end of the fourteenth century it had fallen into disuse, except in rare cases. (See 'le Shallowe' below, p. 45).

Employment of the article not being confined to French words, *le* practically became an English word (*e.g.* le Timbermonger, Surr. 1200, Cur. Reg. R.); le dumbe man, Dev. 1670, Assizes 23/1; see p. 167 below). The article was used in most irregular and uncertain fashion, the commonest practice being to write *la* with natural objects when following *de*, as de la Combe, de la Stone, de la Orchard, etc., and *le*, when following other prepositions, as 'in le Fenne', en le Dene, but exceptions in both cases can be found. For characteristic and

[1] *E.H.S.*, p. 173.

occupational names of males, *le* became usual, and for similar names of females, *la*, but no fixed rule was recognised, and so appears, Stephanus la Wayte, Alicia le Palmer, etc. The forms *li* and *a la* are rare, as Hugo li Baylgy (1275), and Robert a la Feld (1275). From a combination of *de* and *le* came *del* and *du*, the latter being scarce in English records.

Le occasionally coalesced with the following word as Lefevre, Lyle, etc., the apostrophe being added sparingly in the fourteenth century, as Roger l'Estrange, 1311 (Cl. R.). Juxtaposition of the article may always be suspected in difficult names with the initial L. The article sometimes appears through misunderstanding or from clerical error, as:—

Godwin le Gidye, Soms. 1276. (Ass. R. 1230, m. 33d.)
Hen. le Shakespere, Staffs. c. 1420. (D.L.30, 231/16, m. 1.)
Rob. le Shallowe, Lond. 1562. (Denization R., C66, 986, m. 12.)

The true English article may be noticed occasionally towards the end of the thirteenth century, as Theobaldus ye Hattere, but the form adopted seems to have been a mere matter of chance: W. fil' Nich'i ye Maystre *v.* W. le Cartewryt, Warw., 1285 (Ass. R. 956, m. 23).

The Preposition de.[1] The Latin preposition *de*, 'of', 'at', 'in', 'from', was preserved in French without change. In the formation of local descriptions the Anglo-Saxons had used the native *aet* and *on*, as well as Latin *apud* and *de*. During the thirteenth and fourteenth centuries *de* was in most frequent employment, often coalescing with the following *le* or *la*, giving the impression that it is French. In an entry like 'de Johanne de la Grene', the preposition in both cases is Latin, and it

[1] *E.H.S.*, p. 174.

must be assumed to be so in del Grene, where *del* is a hybrid. Des (*de les*) occurs rarely in English records.

De is sometimes duplicated, as Thom. de Deyville, Bucks. 1271 (Ass. R. 60, m. 16) or W. de Daiete,[1] Hertf. 1203 (Cur. Reg. R.); and is also to be found entered in error.

Godel de Brixi, Kent, 1086. (Dom. Bk.) Beorhtsige, a personal name.
John de Longespey, Bucks. 1261. (Ass. R.58, m. 22d.)
Geof. de Calfhird, Cumb. 1292. (Ass. R. 136, m. 1d.)
Thom. de Longespy, Yorks. 1355. (G.D. 141a, m. 1d.)
Hen. de Shakespere, Staffs. 1428. (D.L. 232/6, m. 3.)

Although de Calfhird is incorrect, yet curiously no mistake occurs in Rob. de Neteshirde, Norf. 1338 (G.D. 49, m. 32), Neatishead being a place in Norfolk. Sometimes an apparently erroneous use of *de* is due to Friesic and Dutch influence, *de* being the definite article.

In French, *de* is sometimes found preceding a personal name, due to ellipsis of *le fils*, in parallel to the loss of *son* in our northern 'John o' Bobby'. De was also wrongly entered for *le* and vice versa, but in a case such as le Fen', the peculiarity may be due to clerical omission of *in*. *De*, *in*, and *ad* were commonly interchangeable, but in translating records it is usual to leave the *de*, owing to the precise English equivalent being uncertain, thus, de Bosco, might be 'of the Wood' or 'Atwood'. It will be realised that *de* is no indication of territorial suzerainty, having been merely part of an address used as a mark of distinction for servile tenant as well as overlord.

Coalescence of preposition and following noun (sometimes with the article) has yielded such names as Deville and Delamotte. A modern tendency is to add an

[1] Also W. de Aiete, on the same roll (cf. *ait*, 'island').

apostrophe, as D'Arcy, D'Eath, or De'ath! Names with initial D, which present difficulty, should always be examined with a view to the possibility of being compounds of preposition and local name. So much uncertainty exists that no argument should be based on one appearance of a name with article or preposition, or from the fact that it has neither.

Names of the Norsemen.[1] After a lengthy period of warfare culminating in their defeat at the Battle of Largs, 1266, the Norsemen ceded the Western Isles and Man to the Scottish Crown. The Orkney and Shetland Islands remained under alien rule until about two hundred years later, and it is believed that the Norse language was spoken there down to the last century. It follows that numbers of the names of Scotland are of Scandinavian origin, such as McCodrum (Guthorm), McCalman (Hjalmund), Lamont (Lagmundr), McLeod (Ljotr), Thorburn (Thorbjörn), and McCorquodale (Thorketil). In England also the Norse element can be traced, among the freemen in York in 1378 being Symon Vendilok (*vendiloka*), John Hayfy (*háfi*), Simon Scaif (*skeifr*), John Catelyn (*ketlingr*), Thomas Storr (*stórr*), Matilda Snere (*snæri*), Thomas Crokebayn (*krákubein*), and William Felagh (félagi).

No certainty attaches to the origin of such names, as they may be also found outside the Scandinavian sphere, thus Felagh occurs in Somerset, 1327, and Catelyn besides signifying 'kitten' is a known variant of Catherine.

Jews in England.[2] The Israelites during their wanderings collected names from many countries in which they found refuge, and by the time they made

[1] *E.H.S.* p. 157.
[2] *E.H.S.*, pp. 147–150.

their first appearance in England some of the appellatives were no longer Hebrew. Although we may run across examples such as Moses ben Isaac (son of Isaac), Miriam bath Jacob (daughter of Jacob), and Benedict Gabbay (treasurer of a synagogue), the secondary descriptions were usually French or Latin, as Manasseh l'Aveugle (the blind), Vives le Remangor (the romancer), Isaac Senex (the old), Jurnet de Norwisz, Abraham filius Avigay (*i.e.* Abigail, sons being commonly called after their mothers).

In the year 1290 the Hebrews of Britain suffered dire disaster, Edward I ordering their banishment, and not until the Commonwealth did the unconverted Jew freely enter England. That, in some cases, the designations introduced by the Israelites remained after the expulsion may be evidenced by the metronymic Lycoricia, probably of Greek origin.[1]

Licoricia, wife of David de Oxonia, Jew, 1251. (Pat. R.)
Cokerel son of Licoricia, Jew, 1255. (Pat. R.)
Licoricia de Claytone, Staffs. 1279. (Ass. R., Divers Co.)
Ralph Licoriz, Staffs. 1324. (Coram Rege R.: Salt Coll. x, 46.)
J. Lycorice, Staffs. 1351. (D.L. 30, 228/5, m. 9.)

Welsh Names and Descriptions.[2] By the Statute of Rhuddlan (1284) Wales became united to England, but for many years there had been intermingling between Cymry and Saxon, and both English and Welsh systems of nominal distinction were already established. Taking the lists of tax-payers preserved for the year 1292, under Rhuddlan (Flint) the names are found to be wholly Latin and French; and contrarily under Pengwern (also in co. Flint) they are entirely Welsh, 79 per cent being genealogical, following the ancient native method (se

[1] *E.H.S.*, p. 339.
[2] *E.H.S.*, pp. 121–7.

above p. 25). These family descriptions are occasionally miniature pedigrees recording three generations, as Yorwerth ap Howell ap Llewelyn, or in the Latin form, 'Cadogan filius Madyn fil' Galfrid', but in some English rolls as many as six generations have been noticed. *Ap* is often written *ab*, *vab*, *fab*, *map*; and *merch* (daughter), becomes through mutation, *ferch*, or *verch*. At a later period the *b* and *p* coalesced with the following appellatives, resulting in such surnames, as Beaven (ab Evan) Price (ap Rhys), etc., and by misunderstanding, Upjohn, and by corruption apparently, Applejohn. In England also, the nature of *ab* being unrecognised, the *b* might be elided, as 'Lodewicus ap Thomas alias dictus Lewes a Thomas' (Midx, 1478; K.B. 29, 113, 18 Edw. 4.).

In Welsh the adjectival distinction usually follows the noun which it qualifies, as Adam ap Llewelyn Vachan (the small), but sometimes it takes precedence, as David ap Gwyn Iuan (fair Evan).

"Like the Romance languages Welsh has lost the distinctive endings of the cases. An interesting grammatical feature which has left its mark on Welsh and Cornish surnames is the sound-change known as mutation, being an assimilation with the object of economising effort in pronunciation. By this process the noun or adjective following a proper noun undergoes soft mutation of the initial consonant, thus in Welsh *p* becomes *b*, *t* becomes *d*, *c* becomes *g*, *b* becomes *f*, *d* becomes *dd*, *ll* becomes *l*, *m* becomes *f*, and *rh* becomes *r*."[1] In Cornish, *b* and *m* become *v*, as does *f*; *d* becomes *th* and *j*; *g* becomes *w*, and so on.[2]

The classification of Welsh descriptions is similar to that adopted for Saxon and Norman, as a few examples will illustrate.

Characteristic descriptions. Bul, Bule (*bwl*, 'round'),

[1] *E.H.S.*, p. 41.
[2] *E.H.S.*, p. 379.

Dou, Dw (*du*, 'black'), Gam (*cam*, 'crooked'), Goch (*coch*, 'ruddy'), Gwethel (the Irishman), Hen (the old), Seys (*sais*, 'Saxon'), Vachan (*bychan*, 'little'; the modern Vaughan, Fawne), Wyn (*gwyn*, 'fair').

Local descriptions. The Latin preposition *de* is generally used, but occasionally *o* is to be found, as o kelly (of the grove). Sometimes the preposition coalesced, as Vrnant (*wr*, 'over'; *nant*, 'brook'), at other times the article, as Ebren (*y pren*, 'the tree').

Genealogical descriptions. Following the English practice of dropping *filius* or *fitz*, a tendency may be noticed in the thirteenth-century Welsh rolls of dispensing with *ap* in patronymics, as Gethin, Oweyn, Seysil, Slemen, Tuder, etc.

Occupational descriptions. Few distinctions of this class are to be noticed, and rarely have they survived as surnames. Barun (*barwn*, 'chief'), Crouther (*crythwr*, 'a fiddler'), Meyr (the steward), Pen (the head), Spedor (*spadwr*, 'a gelder'), and Turnaur (*turniwr*, 'a turner'), are among the most prevalent.

Gaelic Descriptions and Surnames.[1] By the treaty of Windsor, in 1175, the head king of Ireland became the liegeman of Henry II, but the natives refused to acknowledge his suzerainty, and resulting from a succession of outbreaks extending over a century, the sphere of English influence became greatly reduced, many Englishmen, moreover, adopting the native language, laws, and customs. It is said that the practice of forming surnames with Ua (or Ó) had ceased before the coming of the English, but that many of the Macs are Englishmen. A restriction on the unpatriotic habit was included in the Statute of Kilkenny (1366) it being ordained that "every Englishman leave off entirely the

[1] *E.H.S.*, pp. 127–9.

manner of naming used by the Irish", from which evidence of a difference between the two methods of nomenclature it may be inferred that the ancient pedigree system yet largely survived.

Norse settlers at an earlier date than the English had adopted the native method, and some of the O-names are Scandinavian, such as Ó hEanraic (O'Henrick), O'hIomhain (O'Hure or Howard). Since, as has been said, some of the Macs are Englishmen too much credence must not be placed in the poetical effusion which commences—"By Mac and O, You'll always know true Irishmen". Under the hands of English and French clerks the O often coalesced with the following name in like manner to the Welsh *ap*, *e.g.* Oconoc (O'Connor), Ocarbri (O'Carbry), etc. Mac is sometimes written Mag before vowels and certain consonants. In Scotland the Gaelic names are very similar to those of Ireland, but in the Lowlands the system corresponded with that current in England.

Internal Racial Movements.[1] One result of the Teutonic conquest was the almost complete elimination of Cymric names throughout the greater part of England. This feature was, however, but a temporary phase, and as conditions became more and more settled so did the movements of the native races increase, many Bretons, Welshmen, and Cornishmen returning to the land of their remote ancestors. One of the uses to which the study of surnames may be put is to trace these migrations, determinable in no other way than by the ethnic adjective.[2] By this means it may be demonstrated that Scotsmen and Irishmen, notwithstanding their love for the fatherlands, spread all over England,

[1] *E.H.S.*, pp. 150–6.
[2] Ewen, *Are the British, "Anglo-Saxons" or Celts?* 1938.

considerable bodies of Welshmen also being identified in Scotland and Ireland. It is estimated that, in 1890, in Ireland there were 50,000 persons bearing the names Wallace, Walsh, and Welsh, and somewhat curiously, in 1865, there were 22,400 residents in Scotland with the family name Scott. That considerable numbers of the migrants retained native names can be evidenced from the parish registers, such as, for instance, those of Ongar (Essex) where the following Welsh surnames can be found:—

Binion, Blyten (Bleddin), Davies, Evans, Ewin, Fuellin (Llewelyn), Gowers, Gryffin, Gualter, Gwin, Jenkin, Jones, Lewis, Lloyd, Meredith, Morice, Onion, Owen, Powel, Price, Reese, Rice, Roberts, Tedder, Tovy (Davy), Traherne, Wallis, Williams.[1]

Distribution of Aliens.[2] The great influence of immigration on the nature of British names has been noticed above, and the preservation of fifteenth-century Subsidy Rolls entirely devoted to the impositions on aliens, enables the distribution of the various races to be ascertained.[3] Rather more than half the foreigners hailed from France and Normandy, their greatest settlements being in Devonshire, Wiltshire, and Kent, three counties also favoured by Flemings. Guernseymen are most noticeable in the first-named county, as are Bretons, who also settled in Cornwall, where they found people who could understand their language. The Irish element became most pronounced in Cornwall, Wiltshire, and Northamptonshire, but Scotsmen, in those days, rarely ventured far south, although two centuries earlier they were quite strongly represented in Paris! Dutchmen or Hollanders became most prominent

[1] *E.H.S.*, p. 206.
[2] *E.H.S.*, pp. 189–93.
[3] The available rolls are but 65 per cent complete.

in Cambridgeshire, Suffolk, Norfolk, and Kent (the Essex rolls not being available). Occasional Spaniards, Portingalers, Manxmen, and others, make up the list of visitors. London, of course, swarmed with aliens from all quarters, and according to the Subsidy Roll of 1540 no less than one-third of the population was foreign, in some parts of the city there being no Englishmen at all! Religious persecution on the Continent in the sixteenth and later centuries caused hordes of foreigners to pour into England, many of whose names are so similar to English words that it is often now impossible to gather from a name whether a family is of native or alien origin.

The following names of strangers, taken from letters of denization and Acts of Naturalisation may have been brought with them or collected on this side, and that numbers of them are actually English is evidenced by White, an appellative borne by German, Frenchman, Norman, Breton, and Spaniard, or Waters, by Dutchman, Frenchman, Spaniard, Belgian, and so on.

Belgium.—Arten, Beeston, Dymock, Taunte, Wensshe.

Brabant.—Brewer, Horne, Rumbalde.

Brittany.—Amber, Asshe, Bras, Bromell, Burdoneck, Cowlande, Creeke, Crowne, Emery, Garrell, Gillett, Griffith, Hamlyn, Harley, Hellyer, Kerver, Pease, Uren.

France.—Aparys, Auger, Bacheler, Barbell, Bawdrie, Belhache, Betune, Boye, Boys, Buller, Capon, Cole, Crekett, Darby, Ducke, Duple, Durban, Durrant, Favell, Ferret, Folliat, Gallapyn, Gallion, Garnyshe, Garvyne, Gascard, Gibbe, Gladde, Grammaire, Gurney, Hackett, Hannock, Harbert, Harden, Helloke, Hewett, Kemmyse, Lavender, Lawner, Longemore, Lorell, Loyall, Manage, Manton, Manyon, Marvel, Morrell, Mounson, Orell, Pallett, Parmenter, Pelter, Pullard, Robie, Sage, Sarasin, Savage, Selleckes, Sister, Snatchall, Strete, Tolmer, Tolmett, Tonny, Udie, Verell, Votier, Vyen.

Gelderland.—Boole, Buckell, Fresshefeld, Harman, Pope.

German Empire (includes Low Countries, etc.)—Barnes, Beche, Belman, Bever, Bowman, Buckett, Clocker, Copperpot, Cowleman, Crust, Draie, Fabian, Fannell, Filde, Fulcote, Fulmer, Hedman, Hodson, Kilgore, Knape, Mallet, Neve, Nutt, Pownce, Purse, Queny, Rawley, Roewell, Rosendale, Rotton, Ryland, Seman, Shredder, Standard, Twyne, Unkles, Wesell.

Germany.—Beake, Blankston, Brekefilde, Hilroad, Kempen, Retters, Rustone, Ryan, Seler.

Greece.—Belle, Benet, Bye.

Holland.—Adrian, Bertye, Cake, Coppinger, Crosse, Fenne, Fulmer, Garrard, Garrison, Hatfeld, Hone, Mase, Nale, Peper, Pole, Ratteler, Water.

Italy.—Barone, Bellin, Binamont, Brime, Cottye, Capon (sometimes *de* Caponis), Doffey, Morando, Spitesa.

Normandy.—Abby, Anderow, Angod, Anthill, Apie, Avenell, Barber, Bartram, Basse, Bellynger, Blanckett, Bowcher, Breake, Brettell, Bygod, Cliffe, Coborne, Codde, Coffyn, Combe, Conscience, Constant, Copie, Counter, Courte, Coven, Dagwell, Deer, Dobye, Dorland, Doute, Drewe, Ellis, Ellyott, Ely, Farryng, Ferys, Fever, Folle, Frye, Gayne, Goolde, Goslynge, Gosse, Grosse, Growte, Harwell, Hayes, Hewland, Heydon, Holland, Holmes, Kenell, Keyne, Mansfelde, Noble, Oger, Patron, Pesant, Provoste, Rawden, Raynes, Rowse, Shipper, Spurre, Stacy, Staffe, Tolarge, Tollett, Valet, Weaver, Wheate.

Picardy.—Allarde, Blanke, Blunte, Caron, Carowe, Dowse, Drawe, Harsent, Kene, Layne, Maister, Motton, Nevell, Powett, Pullett, Turke.

Portugal.—Brothow, Vaiz.

Prussia (Duchy of Cleves)—Cheritree, Clinke, Cocke alias Hane, Crayne, Cristecupp, Cupper, Dam, Dylle, Fysher, Huberd, Kenton, Kytson, Lawe, Meadman, Ryder, Saltpetre, Tillman, Tucker.

Saxony.—Brande, Rippe, Rynge.

Scotland.—Abber, Abercromy, Benefice, Blair, Borne, Boyfeld, Christie, Cockbourne, Conningham, Copelande, Couldwell, Crale, Crayford, Cundalle, Dakin, Dixson, Donaltson, Donckan, Durett, Frebaryn, Frude, Gorden, Gray, Harper, Hay, Hoode, Hume, Inglishe, Irlande, Knokes, Kyle, Loggyn, Lore, Mawcombe, Melin, Methwyn, Moncrif, Myne, Penyton, Ryall, Sincler, Storye, Wodirspone.

Spain (Dominion)—Ackerman, Apple, Archer, Bateman, Batter, Beamonde, Becke, Benson, Best, Breckpot, Brickstone, Bully, Busse,

Calvart, Carioun, Cawell, Corbell, Cotton, Countye, Crafte, Cromer, Dodd, Downett, Fenton, Foe, Forman, Foxe, Kester, Keyser, Leaman, Marston, Maye, Moss, Mullett, Pettye, Playce, Porter, Powles, Raynes, Revett, Ruttey, Sandford, Seres, Sergeant, Sheers, Spinosa, Stoope, Witte.

This list,[1] although but a five per cent selection, vividly illustrates a most important phase in the history of British nomenclature, and is more emphatic than a chapter of assertion in demonstrating how mistaken one may be in visualising from a modern designation of English appearance a long line of English ancestry, and a glance will show that many present-day bearers of what are apparently good old English surnames, must have derived from families of foreign origin, with no great antiquity in this country. In some cases, possibly, the bearers were Englishmen born abroad, but in the majority of these instances they were foreigners who had either taken English names or whose names had become assimilated to some English word. It is manifest that in a consideration of the appellatives of the southern counties of England, in particular, the greatest circumspection must be exercised in determining origin, and that in all cases it is most essential to work out the genealogy of the family before fixing an etymology or deciding on the nationality.

[1] Huguenot Society, vol. VIII, ed. by W. Page, 1893. I gave another list of about 350 names from this source in *E.H.S.*, pp. 201–2.

CHAPTER IV

EVOLUTION OF SURNAMES

Derivative Surnames.[1] Surnames were once words, and evolution is an appropriate term for those processes of expansion, contraction, and internal or orthographic development the original vocable underwent before reaching the final and permanent forms now appearing in the directories.

A surname may be a simple stem, as Young or Duff (*dubh*, Ir. 'black'); a derivative word, as Furb-er (the burnisher); a compound word, as Gate-house; a derivative name, as Hignett (from Richard), or Fr. Niel (from Daniel); a corruption of a name, as Oldman and Blinkinship, from Oldham and Blenkinsop, both originally place-names; or it may be a slight deviation from a simple stem, compound, or derivative, when it is commonly called a variant. It may, of course, be a translation or supposed translation from one language to another, when it may undergo a complete change of most perplexing nature. (See the cases mentioned below, p. 89). Specific technical terms are applied to the various formations.

(i) *Derivatives by addition* (*a*, Initial; *b*, Medial; *c*, Final).

(*a*) Prothesis is the addition of one or more letters or syllables at the beginning of a word or name, as Sturgis

[1] *E.H.S.*, pp. 271–3.

for Turgis (gen.), Stubney for Tubney in Berks, 1200 (Cur. Reg. R.), and probably Spearpoint for Pierpoint (loc.).

Cf. Alan Pinch or Spinc, Cambs. 1204–5. (Cur. Reg. R.)
Ric. Purdaunce or Spurdaunce, Norf, 1403–33. (Blomefield, iii, 126, 134.)
Thom. Kynaston or Akeneston, Shrops. 1509. (Pard. R.)

Prothetic name-formation is very noticeable in the composition of diminutives or hypocorisms (pet-names) of forenames, which have often become surnames. The most used letters are the dentals (*t*, *d*, *n*), as in Ted from Edward, Dandie from Andrew, and Numps from Humphrey.

(*b*) Epenthesis is the interposition of additional letters or syllables in the middle of a word or name. Examples of such intrusion are:—

b after *m*, as in Jambe (Hund. R. 1275), Tomblin, Timbs, Gambling (*i.e.* Gamelin).
d after *n*, as in Hendry (1372, Cl. R.), Grindrod (Greenroyd), Standeley (Stanley).
g after *d*, as in Woodger (the woodman).
g after *n*, as in Mayngwaryng (1509, Pard. R.), Hegingbotham (*Ibid.*)
p after *m*, as in Brompfeld, Glouc. 1291 (G.D.89, m. 2d.), Empson.
n before *g*, as in Messenger, Pottinger.

A curiosity is Rob. Wydowdson, Derb. 1539 (K.B. 9, 541, no. 147), actually either 'the son of the widow' or 'the son of Guy (Wido)'. Intrusive vowels also appear, as Jack(a)way and Bow(y)er.

(*c*) Epithesis or paragoge is the addition of one or more letters or syllables at the end of a word or name. Into this important division fall diminutives and augmentatives, as Dick-ie, Tom-kin, Rich-on, Sand-y (from Sander *i.e.* Alexander) K.B. 29, 142, m. 17. Such names may be called hypocorisms.

Of epithetic type are variants formed by excrescency, but such names are often indistinguishable from normal forms, *e.g.*:—

-*b*. Hugh Columb or Cullum, Dev. 1509 (Pard. R.).

-*d*, as in Hammon-d, Simmon-d, also sometimes variants of the O.E. personal names Heahmund and Simund. Undoubted examples of epithesis are provided by: "William Hamound atte Cherche son and heir of Hamo atte Cherche," Surr. 1317 (Anc. D., A 8034). "Simone fil' Rog'i Simond," Warw. 1346 (Ass. R. 1393 b).

-*g*. Early examples seem to be indistinguishable from O.E. -*ing*-names, but an exception may be Luveking (1190-1, Leic. Pipe R.) Undoubted examples are common in the fourteenth and later centuries: Rog. Crispyng, Norf. 1402 (K.B.9, 190, no. 16).

-*p*. J. in le Holmp, Cambs. 1275 (Hund. R.); Adam de Brom or Bromp, Ire. 1299 (Just. R.)

-*s*, also appears to be excrescent on occasion, but its ground for existence is indistinguishable from other causations (see pp. 134-5).

-*t*, as a variant of -*d*. Ric. Yevaunte (for Welsh Yevan or Evan), Kent, 1509 (K.B.29, 142, m. 35).

(ii) *Derivatives by subtraction* (*a*, Initial; *b*, Medial; *c*, Final).

(*a*) Aphæresis is the falling away or suppression of one or more letters or syllables at the beginning of a word or name. Examples of such diminished names are common: Eng.: Pickernell from Spigurnell, Strange from Lestrange, Damme from Adam, Nash (atten-ash), Twells (at-wells). Manx; Costean from MacAustin, Quilliam from MacWilliam, Gummery from Montgomery. Ir.: Ryan from O'Mulryan. Fr.: Billard from Robillard. Flem.: Tieu from Matthew. Heb.: Jamin from Benjamin. Such names are frequently hypocorisms, but a lengthy name was often shortened for convenience.

W. Kelly or Nanskelly or Lankelly, Cornw. 1434. (K.B.29, 91. Trin. 12 Hen. 6).

W. Worthy or Cokworthy, Lond. 1448. (K.B.29, 91, Hil. 26 Hen. 6.)

Guy Bryght or Gesebryght, Lond. 1468. (K.B. 29, 113, Hil. 7 Edw. 4.)

Hen. Baron or Blakbaron, Lond. 1468. (K.B.29, 113, Mich. 8 Edw. 4.)

Rob. Blanderhasset or Hassett, Warw. 1504. (K.B.9, 433, no. 21.)

J. Slacok or Cok, Norf. 1509. (Pard. R.)

W. Goldsmyth or Smyth, Glouc. 1509. (Pard. R.)

Margaret Wodde or Underwode, Warw. 1509. (K.B.29, 142, m. 40d.)

G. Frankeland alias Frank, Westm. 1655. (C5, 23, 80.)

The gradual and unintentional loss of a short unaccented vowel at the beginning of a word is called aphesis (N.E.D.), as Squire for Esquire, Potecary for Apothecary. Some etymologists make no distinction between aphæresis and aphesis.

(*b*) Syncope or syncopation is the omission of one or more letters or syllables in the middle of a word or name, as Browley for Brodley, Widicote for Wildicote, Brofield for Bromfield, Youngsband for Younghusband.

J. le Walkere or Wakar, Warw. 1339. (Ass. R. 1400, m. 148d.)

Ric. a Carleton or Carlyngton, Midx. 1477. (K.B.29, 113, Mich. 17 Edw. 4.)

J. Rygges or Rygehous, Norf. 1478. (G.D.210, m. 8.)

J. Ulston or Ulveston, Suff. 1509. (Pard. R.)

Thom. Wenley or Wennesley, Derb. 1509. (Pard. R.)

Ric. Cayham or Came, Leic. 1509. (Pard. R.)

Examples of double syncopation are:—Swetnam for Swet(e)n(h)am, Wyndam for Wy(mu)nd(h)am.

(*c*) Apocope is the cutting off or omission of the last letter(s) or syllable(s) of a word or name, as Robb from Robert, providing a third example of hypocorism.

Ric. Penke or Pynkhill, Staff. 1414. (G.D.195, m. 59.)
J. Whyting or White, Yorks. 1441. (G.D.212, m. 6.)
J. Broune or Brounyng, Dev. 1455. (K.B.29, 91, Trin. 33 Hen. 6.)
Awin Walsshe or Owin Walssheman, 1473. (K.B.29, 113, Hil. 12 Edw. 4.)
W. Grenesy or Grenesyde, Norf. 1475. (K.B.29, 113, East. 15 Edw. 4.)
Thom. Kele or Keelhog, Bucks. 1551. (K.B.9, 580, no. 159.)
Thom. Hendry or Hendringham, Norf. 1642. (Chanc. 391/91).

Apocopation is not unusual in Ireland, the Registrar-General in 1890, noted Free for Freeman, Pender for Prendergast, Turk for Turkington (in Belfast and Antrim),[1] and others.

(iii) *Derivatives by mutation* (*a*, Initial; *b*, Medial; *c*, Final).

(*a*) Initial change: as in Vaughan, Fawn; Thrip, Phripp, Fripp; Evan, Fevan, Heven, Ievan, Jevan, Shevan, Yevan, and Zevan, few of which, fortunately, have been preserved. Hypocorisms often evidence mutation, as Peg from Margaret, Bob, Dob, Hob, from Robert, etc., giving such surnames, as Peggs, Bobbett, Dobbie, Hobbs, etc.

(*b*) Medial change; as Finnemore to Phillimore.

(*c*) Final change: as Bertram to Bertrand.

Terms sometimes used are assimilation and dissimilation.

Assimilation is the action by which two unlike sounds become like, as Cob-bold from God-bold, Brat-ton from Bram-ton, and Straf-feld from Strat-feld.

Dissimilation is the action by which two identical sounds become unlike or two similar sounds diverge, as Landsworth from Nansworth, Bransom from Branson.

(iv) *Derivatives by transposition.*

[1] Prof. Weekley, in the rôle of critic (*Observer*, 6 Sept., 1931), makes the extraordinary assertion that "such a shortening of a surname as Turkington into Turk is without example"!

(*a*) Metathesis is the interchange of position between letters or sounds in one syllable of a word or name. Examples of such transpositions are:—Brightwine from Beorhtwine, Throp from Thorp, etc.

J. Curle fil' Petri Crulle, Suff. 1470. (G.D. 209, m. 18.)
W. Gascoign or Gascoyng, Yorks. 1509. (Pard. R.)
Double transposition:—
P. Fairbairn or Frebaryn, a Scot, 1549. (Pat. R.)

(*b*) Hyperthesis is the transposition of a letter from one syllable of a word or name to the preceding or following syllable, or it may be the transposition of two syllables in a word or name. Examples of this form of inter change are Crellin for Crennell (Manx); Talebot to Tabelot (1247, Ass. R. 56, m. 1*d*.). A remarkable example occurs in the Richmond (Surrey) parish register. 1719/20, 2 Jan. J. Pricklove, son of John, bapt. (p. 137); 1720, 25 Nov. J. Loveprick, a child bur. (p. 296).

Greg. Tresahar of Trehasar, Cornw. 1475. (K.B.29, 113, East. 15 Edw. 4.)
Marg. Barty or Batry, Ess. 1509. (Pard. R.)

(v) *Derivatives by composition.*

Parathesis is the juxtaposition of two words without change, as Iron-monger, or Kirk-wood, the hyphen not being used in surnames.[1]

Suffixes in Name-formation.[2] The Indo-European languages are prolific in epithetic modifications, but it is not always possible to distinguish a suffix from a vocable forming a member of a compound name,

[1] For some notice of 'Shake-speare' and a few other hyphenated examples, see my paper in *Baconiana*, June 1936, p. 183.
[2] *E.H.S.*, . 274.

thus *cock* may be a diminutive suffix in Alcock, but a substantival element in Atcock. Suffixes not only have diminutive, but also augmentative force, and others again merely form hypocorisms. British surnames, being derived from words of numerous tongues, exhibit a most interesting variety of suffixes.

Teutonic Suffixes. The principal Anglo-Saxon formations are with an *l*-suffix, as *-il*, *-el*, *-ul*, *-ol*, *-(i)la*, *-ula*, *-ella*, *-ele*, *e.g.* Mannel, Witil; with a *k*-suffix, as *-ic*, *-uc*, *-oc*, *-(i)ca*, *-uca*, *-eca*, *e.g.* Dunnic, Hwituc; with suffixes *-ig*, *-i(g)a*, *-n-*, *-ede*, *e.g.* Ludig, Monnede. In the thirteenth century names with *l*, *k*, and *g*-suffixes were all in use. Such a range of derivatives may be noticed, as Bule—Bullek, Bullig, Bulloc, Bullog, Bullok, Bulluc, and also Bulet and Buletel.

The *k*-suffixes were extensively employed by the Teutons in the formation of hypocorisms or diminutives, *-ka* and *-ko* being noticed as early as the fourth century, and *-kin*, a probable derivative, in the eighth century. The diminutive suffix *-kin* had a great influence in the formation of English surnames, occurring in personal names in pre-Conquest days, and in surnames as Wilkin, Luveking, probable importations from the Low Countries, in the twelfth century. The Subsidy Rolls of 1327 show *-kin*-surnames to have been most prevalent in Suffolk, Kent, and somewhat surprisingly in Gloucestershire, and by the fourteenth century they had reached Wales, as Deikin, Jankin, and even Thloikyn (*i.e.* Lloydkin). The suffix, as *-quin*, was very scarce in French surnames.

Both suffixes *-ke* and *-kin* may be found joined to first or second element of a compound name, as Wil-helm—Wil-ke—Wil-kin; and Jo-han—Han-ke—Han-kin. The suffix *-kin* (or rather *-kins*) was corrupted into *-kiss*, giving such variants as Hotchkiss, Perkiss, Watkiss, and an intrusive *s* has resulted in such absurd names as Bukkeskin, Doggeskin, etc. This very accommodating termination could be added or thrown off as desired.[1]

Joan Syms or Symkyns, 1468. (K.B.29, 113, Hil. 7 Edw. 4.)
Ric. Hoggekyns or Hogges, Midx. 1471. (K.B.9, 332, no. 19.)
The popular termination could also add a French suffix.
W. Wilkynet, Derb. 1330. (G.D.123, m. 18d.)

As late as the seventeenth century -kin is found interchangeable with -son.

Rob. Symson alias Sympkin, Kent, 1610. (K.B.Doggett, 1358, m. 42.)

The Element or Suffix -cock.[2] A purely English termination is *-cock*, but as to its nature, opinions vary, some supposing it to be a hypocoristic and diminutive suffix, others, a complete and significant word in itself, and, therefore, an element or theme of a compound. In point of fact, derivation was due to a number of different processes, and in the *History of Surnames* no fewer than sixteen possibilities were presented, which, providing as they do an excellent illustration of the difficulties facing the student of British surnames, may be repeated with necessary changes.

(i) *Characteristic.* The possibility of *-cock* being the result of a nickname is illustrated by a story told by Jas. Lackington (*Memoirs*, 13th ed. p. 33). The old clerk at Langford, near Wellington (Somers.) "having one Sunday slept in church, and dreaming that he was at a cock-fighting, bawled out, 'a shilling upon the red cock'.

[1] For a full account of suffixes *-ke* and *-kin* in English surnames, see *E.H.S.* pp. 275–82.
[2] *E.H.S.*, pp. 282–8.

And behold the family are called Redcock unto this day."

(ii) *Local.*

(*a*) Corruption of *cot*, 'a small shelter or hut.' Common variants are Woodcock and Woodcot. Thomas de Hancoc is, however, genealogical, occurring as Thomas Hancoc elsewhere.

(*b*) Corruption of *oc.* This suffix following *k*-sound may give *cock*, as layc-ock, 'the small lake' (cf. *layk*, 16th c., N.E.D.)

(*c*) Personal name. In some place-names *-cock* is the personal name, forming an 'inversion-compound', due to Celtic influence, introduced by the Scandinavians, as in Salcock or Sawcock (O.N. *salr*, 'hall'), signifying Cock's hall (A. H. Smith, *Saga Book of the Viking Soc.*, x, pt. ii, p. 203).

(*d*) W. 'cuckoo'. Pennicook from Penicuik (Scotl.) was originally *pen y cog*, 'cuckoo hill'.

(*e*) Element of a prepositional compound.

David Attekokes, Norf. 1275. (Hund. R.)
Ralph Atecock, Lond. 1282. (Will, Ct. of Husting: R. R. Sharpe.)
Rob. Atkoc, Staff. 1332–3. (Subs. R.), but cf. Atkin (*ibid.*).
Possible confusion with Adcock.

(iii) *Genealogical.*

(*a*) O.E. personal names Cocca and Cogga may possibly exist as second elements of compound surnames, cf. Swetcoc (Cambs., 1275) and Cokswete (Ess. 1509, Pard. R.). Bilcock, Telcock, and numbers of other surnames, have common O.E. protothemes.

(*b*) Corruption of *-god.* Algod becomes Algot and Alcot (Dom. Bk.), and a step further would make it Alcok.

(*c*) Corruption of *-cot* (Jewish). Swetecota, a Jewish

feminine name (1288, Cl. R.) would almost certainly become Swetecock, in fact, Bardsley so prints it (Swetcoka).

(iv) *Occupational.*

(*a*) Watchman; (*b*) Leader; (*c*) Cook. It is to be expected that one or other of these vocations has, by parathesis, become a component in surnames (cf. the examples below, p. 151). Swetecok might well be the medieval pastrycook, or Hallcok, 'the hall cook,' but there is no evidence to offer.

Ric. le Personescok, Cambs. 1312. (Pat. R.)
Ric. the grangecok, Northants. 1313. (K.B.27, 214, 31d.)
W. le Yongecok, Worc. 1324. (K.B.27, 258, m. 151.)

(v) *Diminutive suffix.*

(*a*) In name-composition *-cock* appears to have the same diminutive force as *-ke* and *-kin*, *e.g.* Han-ke, Han-kin, Han-coc; Jan-ke, Jan-kin, Jan-cock; but unlike *-ke* and *-kin*, *-cock* is rare in Continental names, and is evidently not of Teutonic or Romance origin.[1]

(*b*) The O.E. suffix *-oc*, to give it an intelligible sound to the modern ear, became *c-oc* and *c-oc-k*, as Balloc, Balcoc; Hwituc, Wytcok; Pilloc, Pylecok, etc.

(*c*) Corruption of Fr. diminutive suffix *-ot* after *k*-sound. Pecoc in Domesday Book may be nothing more than Pecot (*i.e.* Picot, now Pigot and Pycock, Leeds).

(*d*) Corruption of Celt. diminutive suffix *-og* in the same manner.

(vi) *Filial desinence.*

The signification of *-cock* extended so far that, if not

[1] For a selection of examples, *E.H.S.*, p. 286.

synonymous with son, it served like *-kin*, as an alternative for that desinence.

"Ric'us Williamson alias dictus Ric'us Wilcok," Midx. 1453. (K.B. 29, 91, East. 31 Hen. 6.)

Affixed in any of the above forms *-cock* has not the antiquity of *-ke* and *-kin*. Hamelecoc, 11th c. and Cristescoc, 12th c. seem to be occupational descriptions. The surname Elcock, in the form Hellecoc, occurs as early as 1202, and by the end of the century the suffix had come into common use. Examination of a large number of surnames with the termination *-cock* shows that, in most cases, the first elements correspond to O.E. protothemes, Baga, Bil, Heathu, Hol, Love, Pil, Pita, Swet, Tella, etc., pointing to the probability of such appellatives having been personal names with diminutive endings. The suffix *-cock*, being a home product, is more wide-spread than *-kin*, but like the latter was found by analysis to be most prevalent in Gloucestershire. Occasionally the apocope *-co* is found, as in that much-misunderstood name Jericho. Symcox and Hitchcox are orthographic variants of Simcocks and Hitchcocks.

Welsh Suffixes. Reference has been made to diminutive endings given to form personal names (p. 23). The masculine *-yn* added to a surname seems to signify much the same as 'junior'. Consecutive entries on the Cheshire Assize Rolls, 16 Edw. II, are David Thloyd and David Thloydyn (Chester 29, 40, m. 17).

French Suffixes.[1] The French diminutive suffixes, according to Brachet, are *-eau*, *-el*, *-elle*, *-et*, *-ette*, *-ot*, *-otte*, and *-on* (with the intercalation of *-er*, *-ich*, *-ill*). Augmentatives are *-ard*, and *-on*. Some of these ter-

[1] *E.H.S.*, pp. 288–9.

minations had great influence in the formation of English surnames, but it must be emphasised that the determination of their nature by inspection is most uncertain. Many names ending in *l* are apocopes, as Ragenal(d), Ringul(f), and the examples following are subject to that possibility.

-al, *-all.* Variants of *-el*, as Randal, Randall.

-ard. Occurs in Nisard (Denis-ard) and the English surnames, Picard and Crockard (cf. Croc), but the suffix is often indistinguishable from other elements.

-at, *-att.* Variants of *-et* and *-ot*, as Dannatt and Wyatt (Guy).

David Hugh alias Huggatt, Glam. Jas. I. (St. Ch. 8, 54, 5.)

-el, *-ell*, *-le.* This suffix may be, in many instances, of O.E. origin. Domesday Book examples are:—Beorhtel (from which Brettell), Fenchel, Pointel, Wadel.

Ric. and J. Bretel, Bucks. Hen. III. (Ass. R. 62, m. 22.) cf. Rob. de Bretel, Kent, 1130. (Pipe R.)

Boydell (Lincs.) is an early local name, as is Pesel (Northants. W. de Pesel, Lincs. 1276; Ass. R. 1222, m. 15d.)

-er. This termination may have a diminutive as well as an agential force, but identification is difficult. Possible examples are Giler (cf. Gile, Gilot, Gilly, etc.) and Pecker (cf. Pec, Pechel, Peket, Pegon, Pecot, etc.).

-et, *-ett.* A very common suffix, as Basset, Blisset, Dowsett (Douce), Kennett, Olivet, Prewett, and Thomasset.

-il. A scarce variant, as Lovill. Achil occurs in Dom.

Bk. Saisil, so popular in Wales, seems to be the Lat. Cæcilius. Burkill (*i.e.* hill) is probably local from Burghill (Heref.) or other place.

-in. Another common suffix. Modern surnames are, Gubbin, Luckin, and Morin, but often acquiring a final *g*, as Perring, they become confused with O.E. *-ing-* names.

-itt. A variant of *-et*, which is not noticed before the seventeenth century. Modern examples are Blewitt, Lovitt, Raffitt, etc.

-on. In some instances this suffix is an augmentative, as Richardon, 'le gros Richard' (Ferriere), but more often it is a derivation from the ancient accusative, as Hues—Huon, Pieres—Pieron, etc. Basson and Guyon are modern representatives.

-ot, -ott. A very common suffix, as in Aylott, Emmot, Gyot, Ingot, Linnott, Wyot, etc.

-ut. A variant of *-ot*, as in Tibbutt.

Double-Syllabled Suffixes.[1] The number of derivative surnames is increased by the use of double suffixes or double-syllabled suffixes in most cases with a double diminutive force, but sometimes with the additional purpose of distinction from someone of the same name, having the effect of our *junior.* Rare in official records of the twelfth century, such variants do not become common until the fourteenth, and generally they are the product of even later years, being often of purely French origin.

l+n	**-al-in**	Thomalyn (Kent, Ric. II, Subs. 123/59, m. 25.)
	-el-in	Walt. Hamelin, Wilts. 1200. (Cur. Reg. R.)
	-ol-in	J. Jakolin, Cambs. 1275. (Hund. R.)
	-el-on	French examples are: Bousselon, Nivelon.
	-il-on	French examples are: Jacquillon, Bancillon.

[1] *E.H.S.*, p. 289.

l+t	**-al-et**	W. Hanalet, Channel Islands, 1309. (Assizes.)
	-el-et	Ralph Hackelet or Hackelette, Heref. 1509. (Pard. R.)
	-ol-et	Rob. Tripolet, Cornw. Mich. 1295. (K.B.27, 147, m. 18.)
	-al-ot	Rus. Robalot, Cambs. 1275. (Hund. R.)
	-el-ot	Rob. Godelot, Bucks, 1257. (Ass. R. 57, m. 11.)
	-il-ot	A French example is Jacquillot.
	-ol-ot	Thom. Bartholot, Cambs. 1275. (Hund. R.)
n+l	**-en-el**	Pet. Tremenel, London. (Coroner's R.)
	-in-el	Greg. Tropinel, Bucks. 1257. (Ass. R. 57, m. 4.)
	-on-el	Ric. Cardonel, Channel Islands, 1309. (Assizes.)
	-en-ol	Rob. Gosenol, Cambs. 1275. (Hund. R.)
	-in-ol	Ric. Dodinol, Salop, 1275. (Hund. R.)
n+n	**-en-in**	The French have Huguenin from Hugues.
n+t	**-en-et**	Ric. Pikenet or Pikenot, Lincs. 1275. (Hund. R.)
	-in-et	Ric. Robynet, Lincs. 1411. (Parl. R.iii, 649.)
	-on-et	Emmelotta Baudonette, Channel Is. 1309. (Assizes.)
	-en-ot	Rad. Wydenot, Bucks. 1271. (Ass. R. 60, m. 27.)
	-in-ot	Hen. Godynot.
r+l	**-er-el**	W. Chickerel, Dors. 1247. (Ass. R. 56, m. 1d.)
r+t	**-er-et**	The French have Jeanneret.
t+l	**-et-el**	Agnes Buletel, Cambs. 1275. (Hund. R.)
t+n	**-ot-en**	W. Emmoten, Warw. 1375. (Subs.)
	-et-in	Geof. Anketin, Ess. 1275. (Hund. R.)
	-ot-in	French examples are Jannotin, Lambotin.
	-ot-on	Adam Tyboton, Warw. 1389. (Ass. R. 1496, m. 34.)
t+t	**-et-ot**	J. Godytot (but cf. Godelot), Beds. 1396. (G.D. 182, m. 15d.)

Derivation by Suffix. The remarkable multiplication of surnames by the use of suffixes, will be illustrated by the derivatives of Richard (Rickard, Rickart, Rickert, Ricard, Ricart, etc.)

Simple pet form: Dick, Hick, Higg, Hitch, Hytche, Rich, Rick; Dickey, Dickie, Dicksee, Dicksie, Dicky, Dixey, Dixie, Hickey, Hickie, Richey, Richie.

Suffix *-cock*: Hickcox, Hickok, Hiscock, Hiscocks, Hiscoke, Hiscox, Hitchcock, Hitchcocks, Hitchcox.

Suffix *-kin*: Confused with *-en*, *-in*. (See below.)

Suffix *-en*: Dicken, Dickens, Diggens, Hichen, Hitchen.

Suffix *-in*: Dickin, Dickins, Diggins, Hickin, Hickins, Higgins, Hitchin, Hitchins, Richin (also a distinct name).

Suffix *-on*: Diccon, Dickons, Diggons, Higgon, Rickon.

Suffix *-et*: Higgatt, Higgett, Ricket, Rickett.

Suffix *-ot*: Higgot, Higgott.

Double diminutives: Diglin, Hicklin, Hignett, Richelot, Rikelot.

Simple genitive: Ricards, Richards, Rickards, Rickarts, Rickerts.

Genitive of diminutives: Dicks, Digges, Diggs, Dix, Hichens, Hichins, Hickes, Hickins, Hicks, Higgens, Higgins, Higgons, Higgs, Hitchins, Hix, Riches, Rickets, Ricketts, Ricks, Rix. (Possibly also Reckitts.)

Filial desinence: Dicconson, Dickason, Dickenson, Dickeson, Dickinson, Dickson, Dixon, Hichinson, Hichisson, Hickson, Higginson, Higson, Hitchinson, Hixon, Hixson, Richardson, Rickartson, Rickatson, Rickerson, Rickertson, Ricketson, Rickson, Rixon.

Corruptions: Dickerson, Hiscott, Record (*i.e.* Rickard).

Confusion occurs with the O.E. personal name Hig (Hyge-), exemplified by Hugh Higge, Lincs. 1273 (Hund. R.), and so also with O.E. Rick, Huchen (*i.e.* Hugh), Richer, and Hitchen (local), but an undoubted variant is Higdon, which is found both as christian and surname.

Higdon de Slynesby, Yorks. 1379. (Poll Tax, p. 239.)

"Ric'us Hogge alit' vocat' Higdon Hogg," Yorks. 1432. (K.B. 29, 91, Mich. 11 Hen. 6.)

Early examples of Hig as a distinct personal name are:

Æthelin Higa, Wilts, 901–24. (Birch Cart. Sax., 591.)
Hig, manumitted serf, Dev. 11th cent. (Thorpe, p. 638.)

CHAPTER V

VARIATION AND CORRUPTION

Orthographic Changes.[1] In the previous chapter consideration having been given to the evolution of surnames and the production of new varieties by acknowledged grammatical processes, attention can now be turned to orthographic variants formed either in accordance with regular laws, or in irregular manner, often with most curious and perplexing results. The signification of surnames of the latter type, in the process of mutation, may also undergo changes of various degrees, which may be classed as follows:—

(i) *Signification retained.* Variation of orthography whereby the original description or surname has received a number of different forms, recognisable as having a common origin, thus Petit, Petitt, Pettit, Pettitt, etc. are all clearly from Fr. *petit*, and Uran, Uren, Urin, Urian, Urion, etc. may be safely derived from the one personal name.

(ii) *Signification lost.* Corruption of orthography whereby the original description or surname has received a sound and form conveying no apparent meaning. Surnames of this type are: Dunbabin, Earp, Gallafent, Kirty, Pagriff, Pemprys, Sumption, Tollemache, etc., the origins and significations of which have yet to be proved.

[1] *E.H.S.*, p. 294.

(iii) *Signification changed.* Corruption of orthography, whereby the original description or surname has so changed as to have received a meaning entirely different from the original signification. A most important influence in name-formation has been the tendency to assimilate a strange and unknown appellative to something which has a familiar signification or is more easily pronounced, regardless of the destruction of the original meaning. Thus the Lancashire local name of Bickerstaff, arriving in the South, its nature unrecognised, was turned into Pikestaff, and due to similar causes Old'am becomes Oldman; Cowherd, Coward; and so on.

"Joh'es Bykerstaf alias dictus Joh'es Pykestaf," Bucks. 1438. (K.B. 9, 230, no. 156.)
W. Wynslade, Wideslade or Widerlade, Dev. 1509. (Pard. R.)

The origin of Metcalf, having hitherto proved baffling, the following series of entries, all taken from one Controlment Roll (K.B. 29, 91), is of considerable interest, clearly proving that, like so many more of the supposed verb-plus-noun nicknames, it is nothing more than a corruption of a local name.[1]

J. Metcroft, outlaw, Lond. 1449. (East 27 Hen. 6.)
J. Medecroft, gent. outlaw, Lond. 1452. (Mich. 31 Hen. 6.)
J. Metcalf, gent. outlaw, Lond. 1453. (Hil. 31 Hen. 6.)
J. Metcalf, outlaw, Lond. 1454. (East. 32 Hen. 6.)

Rog. Medcalf, outlaw, Yorks. 1452. (Hil. 30 Hen. 6.)

Thom. Medycrofte, gent. outlaw, Lond. 1451. (East. 29 Hen. 6.)
Thom. Metcalfe, gent. outlaw, Lond. 1453. (Trin. 31 Hen. 6.)

This excellent illustration paves the way to the realisa-

[1] The surname occurs in 1379 as de Meducroft in Tinsley, West Riding (Yorks. Arch. Soc., V, 242) and Miducroft in Thorpesalvayne, West Riding (*Ibid.* V, 256).

tion that there is nothing extraordinary in Anthill from Ampthill, Barefoot from Barford, Egg from Edge, Fairbrass from Ferbras (iron-arm), Greedy from Gredhay, Heron from O'Ahern (Ir.), Physick from Fishwick, Stockhole from Stockhall, Swanshead from Swineshead, or Joyberd, Greenhouse and Flute from the Welsh Iorwerth, Goronwy and Lloyd.

In the same way that we twist names so do other nationals. Baring Gould noted a case in which the Cornish Pengelly (the head of the grove) was changed into Pain-au-lait. This peculiarity raises an important point for consideration since curious French and German names are sometimes cited to uphold, by supposed analogy, strange English nicknames, whereas in all probability they are likewise corruptions. No statement on the origin of a modern name can be considered final without support from a series of dated and localised examples. Numbers of so-called nicknames were nothing more than manufactured appellatives, thus a foundling might be called Coalhouse or Simon Jude, a Jew might add to his attractions the label Veilchenduft (scent of violets) or Schmetterling (butterfly); and many curiosities resulted from the Act of Parliament, 1465, enforcing Irishmen within the Pale to take English surnames.

Influence of Palæography.[1] The sources from which early surnames may be obtained are manuscript records, but even where these are contemporary, the correct orthography is not always preserved, and for that difficulty there is little or no remedy, unless other examples of the name can be found, or the words forming it be identified. This want of a standard orthography combined with misreading by copyists has led to many

[1] *E.H.S.*, pp. 294–8.

strange variants becoming handed down in lists of names, and the danger of basing an argument on one example is manifest,[1] thus in an Elizabethan index to patents, occurs Shappere, which investigation shows should have been Shaxpere, a form of Shakespere. The *x* and *p* were often indistinguishable, and so also *c* and *t*, *e* and *o*, *lk* and *w*, and so on. Names like Menzies, Dalziell, ffiske,[2] and Smijth, have features resulting from misreading, and difficulties constantly occur with such names as Lone and Love, Acworth and Atworth, Elkin and Ewin, Dyn and Oyn, etc. The medieval scribe was frequently misled by his brethren, with resulting confusion, as exemplified by the following extracts.

Rog. Vyner alias dictus Rog. Wyver, Glouc. 1451. (K.B.29, 91, East. 29 Hen. 6.)

Ric. Geyke alias dictus Ric. Geyte, Lond. 1456. (K.B.29, 91, Mich. 35 Hen. 6.)

Ric. Rigby alias dictus Ric. Riggeley, Midx. 1458. (K.B.29, 91, Hil. 36 Hen. 6.)

An inexperienced transcriber should take the precaution of carefully studying the writing of his period, otherwise there is a tendency to take the names to be what they appear to the modern eye, with very unfortunate results, as will be illustrated below (p. 176).

Corrupt Orthography.[3] The spoken alphabet of English contains forty-three sounds: to represent them the written alphabet has only twenty-six letters (of which five, namely c, q, x, w, and y, are superfluous). One sound may be written in different ways, as long *a* in f*a*te, br*ai*d, s*ay*, gr*ea*t, n*eigh*, pr*ey*, g*ao*l, g*au*ge; and one symbol may be given different sounds, as in bough,

[1] See preface, p. 8.
[2] Dekker, *Westward Hoe*, 1607, ii, 1, makes Justiniano, a writing-master, in discussing a pupil's progress, refer to 'double F' and 'double LL'.
[3] *E.H.S.*, p. 298.

cough, dough, hiccough (=cup), hough (=hock), tough, through, thorough. "It is, however, in the vowel sounds that the irregularities of our alphabet are most discernible. Thirteen vowel-sounds are represented to the eye in more than one hundred different ways."[1]

The difficulties in spelling English words are appreciated by all, and to correctly set down a dictated name, which may be in any one of half a dozen unknown languages is much more likely to yield curious results. In the days before surnames had acquired a permanent character few men could write or spell, the clerk being left to follow his own fancy, which was seldom consistent; for instance, in one list of homagers at Flint, in 1344, the name Yevan appears in no fewer than nine different forms. Fifty orthographic variants of one appellative are frequently to be traced in old records, and in some cases, as Mannering, Ewen, and Cushion, from one to five hundred may be found. The writer has noticed his own name written with from three to nine letters, as Eun, Ewen, Ewing, Ewinge, Ewinges, Hewinges, and Hewghinge, the spelling in a Norfolk will, and even longer forms would not be impossible for a medieval scribe. So many variants being prevalent, it will be readily understood, that not only in distant parts of the country, but in the same family, different forms might become fixed, and in this way the diversity of surnames vastly increased.

The Aspirate.[2] The number of surnames is enlarged by irregularity in the use of the letter *h*; thus an initial may be dropped, as Urlwin for Herlewin, or a medial omitted, as Oldum for Oldham, but a more numerous class of surnames is formed by prefixing an initial *h*, as

[1] J. M. D. Meiklejohn, *The English Language*, 1886, p. 8.
[2] *E.H.S.*, pp. 301–6.

Hadkins for Adkins, Haskew for Askew, or aspirating the second syllable, as Owhen for Owen, Hewhet for Hewett, Langhaker for Langaker, or even both elements, as Howhen.

Casual use of the letter *h* is of great antiquity, being adversely commented upon by Roman writers, and in Anglo-Saxon charters, it may be noticed, it is widespread. Aspiration, meaning here prefixion of the initial letter *h*, so far as it has affected the names of persons, is shown by an analysis of 100,000 names to have been of steady growth, varying from 17 per cent of the total number of appellatives commencing with A,E,I,O,U,Y, and H, in pre-Conquest days, to about 40 per cent in 1275, finally rising to about 54 per cent. The greatest proportion of H-names was found to be in the counties of Cornwall and Devon.

The use of the initial H is much greater in surnames than in dictionary words, and this condition is believed to be due to the large number of family designations derived from localities, which names show a high proportion beginning with H, but the explanation of that feature must be left to the student of place-names.

The modern consonantal digraph *wh* appears in the rolls towards the end of the twelfth century, but the O.E. spelling was not entirely displaced for two centuries, the four forms, Hw, W, Qw, and Wh, being used concurrently. Some examples of aspiration may be noticed.

W. le Wrhyte, Ess. 1282. (G.D. 18a, m. 33.)
Hen. Nhytyngale, Oxf. 1294. (G.D. 95, m. 10.)
W. Fwelewryght, Irel. 1306. (Just R.)
W. Hwitheued, Kent. 1318. (G.D. 27, m. 26.)
Steph. le Nhesse, Dors. 1327. (G.D. 120, m. 14.)
Thom. Hushbonde, Leic., 1346. (Ass. R. 1433, m. 78.)

Kat. de Whale, Westm. 1359. (G.D. 141a, 48d.)
"Ric'o of yhe Cloude" Warw. 1368. (Ass. R. 1472, m. 21d.)
J. Wehbbe, Bucks. 1386. (G.D. 14, m. 12.)
J. Whalsheman, Warw. 1395. (Cor. R. 192, m. 2.)
J. Snowhwyte, Warw. 1397. (Cor. R. 192, m. 8d.)
J. Voughwhan (Vaughan), Suff. 1467. (G.D. 207, m. 9d.)
Thom. Whightacres, Herts. 1495. (K.B. 29, 139. Mich. 11 Hen. 7.)

In some cases the addition or loss of *h* has quite altered the meaning of a name, *e.g.* Blackhall became Blackall, Urry and Hurry were interchangeable, and Sharpharowe has been written for Sharparrow.

Common Equations.[1] The endless variation in the orthography of surnames, briefly mentioned above, may now be exemplified. All vowels were interchangeable, even as late as the sixteenth century.

Initial: a=e=i=o: J. Aweyn, Ewayn, Iwayn, or Owayn, Ess. 1339–57. (Halstead Court Rolls.) Ywayn is also an early Essex form.
Medial: a=e=o=y: J. Wellet, Willet, Wellot, Wyllot, Surr. 1509. (Pard. R.)
a=e=i=y=u: W. Turwhatt, Turwhet, Turwhite, Tyrwhyt, Lincs. 1509. (Pard. R.)
Final: a=e=ey=ow=y: W. Bulla, Bulle, Bulley, Bullow, or Bully, London, 1509. (Pard. R.)

The result of this casual orthography may be illustrated by the modern surname Tibbatts, Tibbett, Tibbitt, Tibbott, and Tibbutt.

It is not practicable to formulate complete laws of variation, covering all districts and periods, so multitudinous are the changes which abound, but a few of the commoner consonantal and diphthongal equations may be noticed.

[1] *E.H.S.*, pp. 306–12.

a=ae=ay. Ric. Panell, Paenell or Paynell, Lincs. 1509. (Pard. R.)
a=au=ou. J. Palet, Paulet or Poulet, Hants. 1509. (Pard. R.)
a=aw=ay. Edm. Ralegh, Rawley, or Rayley, Dev. 1509. (Pard. R.)
a=ie=ou. W. Tailar, Taillier or Taillour, Staffs. 1509. (Pard. R.)
a=in, as in Pottager, Pottinger.
ai=ey. J. de Staingreve or Steyngreve, 1295. (Inq. p.m.)
al=au. Nich. Calvell' or Cauvell, Glouc. 1205. (Cur. Reg. R.)
an=er. W. Harman or Harmer, Norf. 1509. (Pard. R.)
an=ham. Geoff. de Dynan or Dynham, 1258. (Inq. p.m.)
au=a (q.v.). **aw=ay=a** (q.v.). **ay=ae** (q.v.).
au=e. Joan Straunge or Strenge, Shrops. 1509. (Pard. R.)
aw=a (q.v.)
awe=o. Rob. Limbawe or Limbo, Hants. 1452. (K.B. 29, 91, Trin. 30 Hen. 6.)
ay=awa (q.v.)
ay=o. Edw. Baynes or Bones, Ess. 1509. (Pard. R.)
b=m. J. Turnebull or Turnmull, Soms. 1509. (Pard. R.)
b=p. Gilb. Brudham or Prudumme, Surr. 1199, 1201. (Cur. Reg. R.); J. Begot or Pegot, Norf. 1471. (G.D. 209, m. 4.); J. Pacon or Bacon, Cornw., Jas. I. (Chanc. Index, p. 47.)
b=v. Derick Obell or Ovyll, Lond. 1509. (Pard. R.)
c=ch. W. Carpe or Charpe, Norf. 1275. (Hund. R.)
c=ck. Laur. de Broc or Brock, Cambs. 1275. (Hund. R.)
c=g=k. J. Cross or Grosse, Norf. 1509. (Pard. R.) ; Thom. Pycot, Pigot or Pykott, Bucks. 1509. (Pard. R.)
c=gh. J. Ughtred or Uctrede, Yorks. 1298. (Inq. p.m.)
c=qu=qw. J. Qwykerell (*i.e.* Cokerell), Lincs. 1453. (Pat. R.); J. Quoniam or Conyam, Dev. 1509. (Pard. R.)
c=s=ss. W. Brice, Brise or Brisse, Dev. 1509. (Pard. R.); Ric. Vecy, Vesy or Vessy, Norf. 1509. (Pard. R.)
c=s=z. Rog. la Cuche, Suche or Zuche, Leic. 1202–3. (Cur. Reg. R.); W. de Baucan or Bauzan, Dev. 1200–1. (Cur. Reg. R.)
ce=s. Hen. Daunce or Dans, Suff. 1509. (Pard. R.)
ch=c. (q.v.)
ch=dg. The flattening of the final sharp palatal was common, as Partriche.
ch=g. W. Aucher or Auger, Kent. 1509. (Pard. R.)
ch=gg. Hen. Rycheman or Riggeman, Hants. 1427. (G.D. 205, m. 6.)
ch=h. see sch.

ch=k. Hugh Richespald or Rikespald, Beds. 1204–5. (Cur. Reg. R.)
ch=sh. J. le Chepherde, Beds. 1316. (G.D.I, m. 19.)
ck=c (q.v.)
ck=gg, as in Black, Blagg, etc.
ckes=x. Duckesworth and Duxworth. (Whalley Par. R.)
d=g. J. Furland or Furlang, Dev. 1509. (Pard. R.)
d=k. Rob. Brudenell or Bryknell, 1509. (Pard. R.)
d=r. Ric. Quadles or Quarles, Midx. 1503. (K.B.29, 139, Hil. 18 Hen. 7.); W. Adams or Aram, Glouc. 1509. (Pard. R.)
d=t. J. Radclyff or Ratclyff, Lancs. 1509. (Pard. R.); Ric. de Herierd or Heriert, Midx. 1200. (Cur. Reg. R.)
d=th. J. Bidlake or Bithelake, Dev. 1509. (Pard. R.); J. Bradford or Bradforth, Yorks. 1509. (Pard. R.)
dg=ch (q.v.)
dg=g=gg. Brugeende, Bruggeend, or Bridgeend.
e=au (q.v.)
e=eau. G. Belser or Beaulsyer, Kent. 1509. (Pard. R.)
e=in=ing. Ric. de Peltedon or Peltindon, 1202–3. (Cur. R.); Hen. Nightegale or Nightyngale, Bucks. 1337. (Ass. R. 73, m. 12d.); Joel de Buketon or Bukyngton, Dev. 1356. (Inq. p.m.)
e=om. Thom. Faukeberge or Faucomberge, Yorks. 1356. (Inq. p.m.)
e=uy. Thom. Gebon or Guybon, Norf. 1509. (Pard. R.)
ea=ew=ou. Humph. Feaster, Fewster, or Fouster, Leic. 1509. (Pard. R.)
eau=e (q.v.)
ee=eigh. W. Rowelee or Roweleigh, Shrops. 1509. (Pard. R.)
ee=owe. W. Barlee or Barlowe, Ess. 1509. (Pard. R.)
eo=u. Nich. de la Huse or de la Heose, Wilts. 1300. (Inq. p.m.)
er=an (q.v.)
er=ier. Ric. Roger or Rogier, Hants. 1509. (Pard. R.) See also p. 152.
er=in. Catterson, Cattinson; Dickerson, Dickinson, etc.
er=on. Ric. Hinder or Hindon, Wilts. 1509. (Pard. R.)
er=re. Hugh de Lowther or Louthre, Cumb. 1317. (Inq. p.m.)
es=s (initial). Pet. Spilleman or Espileman, 1292. (Inq. p.m.)
ew=ou=ea (q.v.)
ewe=ui=u, as in Brewes, Bruis, Brus, etc.
ey=ai (q.v.)
ey=o. W. Breteyn or Breton, Lond. 1509. (Pard. R.)
ey=owe. J. Wensley or Wenslowe, Yorks. 1509. (Pard. R.)

f=p. Rob. Gefson or Jepson, Yorks. 1509. (Pard. R.)

f=ph. J. Profete or Prophete, Bucks, 1382. (G.D. 14, m. 19.); W. Phethorston (Featherstone), Notts. 1382. (Ass. R. 1496, m. 95.)

f=v.—Marmaduke Fag son of J. Vag, Somers, 1361. (Inq. p.m.): W. Venell or Fenell, Norf. 1471. (G.D. 209, m. 4.)

f=w. W. Wymondesfold or Wymondeswold, Notts, 1509. (Pard. R.)

Fl=Ll=Thl. Lloyd and Llewelyn in the mouths of Englishmen become Floyd and Thlewelyn.

ft=t. Thom. de Lovetoft or Lovetot, Hunts. 1319. (Inq. p.m.)

g=c (q.v.); **g=ch** (q.v.); **g=d** (q.v.); **g=dg** (q.v.)

g=j=y. Thom. Folgambe, Folejambe, or Folyambe, Derb. 1509. W. Geffrey or Jeffrey, Lond. 1509. (Pard. R.)

g=k=c (q.v.); **gg=cc** (q.v.); **gg=ch** (q.v.); **gg=ck** (q.v.); **gg=g=dg** (q.v.)

gg=k. Hen. Briggis or Brykys, Lond. 1509. (Pard. R.)

gg=ng. Matilda Riggebelle and Ric. Ringebelle, Suff. 1275. (Hund. R.)

gh=c (q.v.)

gh=th. W. de Brighnothe or Brithnothe, Lond. 1337. (Cor. R.)

gh=w. W. Senagh or Senowe, Heref. 1509. (Pard. R.)

gh=y. Thom. de Huntelegh or Hunteleye, 1354. (Inq. p.m.)

ght=ch (q.v.)

ght=t. Ric. Schipwryte, Cambs. 1275. (Hund. R.); Mod. Shipwright.

gu=gw=w. Ric. ap Gualter or Walter (also occ. Gwalter), Wales, 1509. (Pard. R.); Thom. Willyam or Gwylyon, Midx. 1475. (K.B.29, 113, 15 Edw. 4.)

gw=qu. Margaret Gwelch or Quelch, 1686–8. (St. James Clerkenwell Par. R.)

h. For notes on the aspirate, see above, p. 76.

h=ch. See **sch.**

h=k. Elena Wolfrich, Rob. Wolfrick, Oxf. 1275. (Hund. R.)

h=w. Thom. Redehood or Redewood, Lond. 1509. (Pard. R.)

ham=man. Adam Walsham or Walshman, Warw. 1367. (Ass. R. 1472, m. 16 *et seq.*)

ham=an (q.v.)

hay=y. Leo Perchay or Percy, Yorks. 1509. (Pard. R.)

hevede=head. See p. 83; **hw=wh.** See above, p. 77.

i=or. Steph. Berwith or Barworth, Berks. 1509. (Pard. R.)

ie=a (q.v.); **ier=er** (q.v.)

ig=y. J. Reignold or Reynold, Wales, 1509. (Pard. R.)
ill=le. Phil. Constable or Constabill, Yorks. 1509.
in=a (q.v.); **in=e** (q.v.); **in=er** (q.v.); **ing=e** (q.v.)
is=y=ys. W. de Suberis, Subery, or Suberys, Cambs. 1275. (Hund R.)
j=y=g (q.v.); **k=ch** (q.v.); **k=d** (q.v.); **k=g=c** (q.v.); **k=gg** (q.v.) **k=h** (q.v.)
kkes=x. Rob. Bekkes or Bex, Cambs. 1509. (Pard. R.)
l=n. J. Fylmore or Fenymore, Dev. 1509. (Pard. R.)
l=r. Hervey Blasard or Brasard, Suss. 1204–5. (Cur. Reg. R.)
l=u, as in *-feld*, *-feud*, etc.
le=ill (q.v.); **Ll=Thl=Fl** (q.v.); **m=b** (q.v.)
m=n. Ric. Gummer or Gunner, Norf. 1509. (Pard. R.); J. Lyngan or Lyngen, Heref. 1509. (Pard. R.)
m=nd. Bertrand or Bertram de Criel, Kent, 1306. (Inq. p.m.)
man=ham (q.v.); **n=l** (q.v.); **n=m** (q.v.)
n=th. Madock ap Griffin or Griffith, 1321. (Inq. p.m.)
n=u. See above, p. 8; **nd=m** (q.v.); **ng=gg** (q.v.); **o=aw** (q.v.); **o=ay** (q.v.); **o=ey** (q.v.)
o=oo=ou=ow. Giles Coper, Cooper, Couper, or Cowper, Dors 1509. (Pard. R.)
o=ogh=ue. Ralph Asco, Ayscogh, or Askue, Chesh. 1509. (Pard R.)
o=ow=u=uy. Thom. Corle, Crowle, Crull, Cruyll, Lond. 1509 (Pard. R.)
o=oy. W. Frosell or Froyzell, Heref. 1509. (Pard. R.)
o=ur. J. Lillebone or de Lilleburne. 1356. (Inq. p.m.)
ogh=o (q.v.)
oi=u. Alex. Boill or Bull, Yorks. 1509. (Pard. R.)
om=e (q.v.); **on=er** (q.v.)
oo=ow, as in Foole and Fowl. (Whalley Par. R.)
oo=u. J. Pooregold or Puregold, 1509. (Pard. R.)
or=l (q.v.); **ou=a** (q.v.); **ou=ew=ea** (q.v.); **ow=oo** (q.v.); **ow =ee** (q.v.); **owe=ey** (q.v.)
ou=owe=u. Rob. Cowerte, Court or Curt, Berks. 1509. (Pard. R
owgh=u. Chr. Owghtred or Utred, Yorks. 1509. (Pard. R.)
oy=o (q.v.)
oy=y. Pet. Boyle or Byle, Hants. 1509. (Pard. R.)
p=b (q.v.); **p=f** (q.v.); **ph=f** (q.v.)
ph=th. W. de Phickebrom (*i.e.* Thickebrome), Staffs. 13th (Salt Soc. xvii, 250.)

ph=wh, as in the Irish names, Phelan, Whelan.
qu=qw=c (q.v.); **qu=gw** (q.v.)
qu=qw=w=wh. Hug. de Wadon or Quaddon, Bucks. 1204. (Cur. Reg. R.); W. Qwyteheued (Whitehead), Cumb. 1300. (G.D. 10a, m. 6.)
r=d (q.v.); **r=l** (q.v.); **r=y** (q.v.); **re=er** (q.v.); **s=ce** (q.v.); **s=es** (q.v.)
s=sc=sh. Osbert de Sipton, Scipton, or Shipton, Glouc. 1201–3. (Cur. Reg. R.)
s=st, as Kelson for Kelston.
s=ts. W. Lyster or Lytster, Yorks. 1509. (Pard. R.)
s=x. Gerard de Ixele or Disel, Northants. 1200–1. (Cur. Reg. R.); Nich. Vaus or Vaux, 1509. (Pard. R.)
s=z=c (q.v.)
sch=sh. Hug. le Schipwryte, Cambs. 1275. (Hund. R.)
sh=ch (q.v.); **sh=sc=s** (q.v.)
sh=tch. Dishborne and Ditchborne. (Grimsby Par. Reg.)
ss=c (q.v.); **st=s** (q.v.)
st=t. Alex. de Oketon or Okeston, Dev. 1276. (Inq. p.m.)
t=d (q.v.); **t=ft** (q.v.); **t=ght** (q.v.); **tch=sh** (q.v.); **th=d** (q.v.); **th=gh** (q.v.); **th=n** (q.v.); **th=ph** (q.v.); **Thl=Fl=Ll** (q.v.); **ts=s** (q.v.); **u=eo** (q.v.); **u=l** (q.v.); **u=n** (q.v.); **u=oi** (q.v.); **u=oo** (q.v.); **u=owe** (q.v.); **u=owgh** (q.v.); **u=ui=ewe** (q.v.); **ue=ogh=o** (q.v.); **ur=o** (q.v.); **uy=e** (q.v.); **uy=o** (q.v.); **v=b** (q.v.); **v=f** (q.v.); **w=f** (q.v.); **w=gh** (q.v.); **w=gw=gu** (q.v.); **w=h** (q.v.); **w=qu** (q.v.); **w=wh** (see above, p. 77).
w=y. W. de Bruwer or Bruyere, Derb. 1275. (Hund. R.)
wh=hw (see above, p. 77); **wh=ph** (q.v.); **wh=w=qu** (q.v.); **x=ckes** (q.v.); **x=kkes** (q.v.); **x=s** (q.v.); **y=gh** (q.v.); **y=hay** (q.v.); **y=ig** (q.v.); **y=j=g** (q.v.); **y=oy** (q.v.); **y=r** (see below, p. 95); **y=w** (q.v.); **y=ys=is** (q.v.)
ys=z. J. Traynez or Trayneys, Yorks. 1311. (Inq. p.m.)
z=c (q.v.); **z=s=c** (q.v.)

This list of equations illustrates some of the principal variations which are to be found in ancient documents, and its value lies in its provision of clues to possible forms of words, thus if Fool=Fowl, in one case, it would be well in making a search for Bowne to also look for Boone. The equations are not, of course, rigidly applicable in every case; period, locality, and the letters preceding or following must all be considered.[1] Errors are often due to failure of ear or eye, and sometimes extend to a whole syllable.

W. Treweblod or Trewebody, Warw. 1317. (K.B.27, 229, m. 45d.)
Rich. Fitzwater or Flewwater,— 1604. (C54, 1770.)
J. Coulbrooke or Couldroppe, Glouc. Jas. I. (Chanc. Index. 347.)
B. Tredwell or Tredwayne, Dev. 1650. (C5, 395, 221.)
J. Seabright or Seaborne, Midx. 1657. (C5, 33, 50.)
Eliz. Stonehouse or Stonestreet, Surr. 1669. (C5, 55, 81.)
R. Cheshire or Chester, Midx. 1709. (C5, 596, 66.)

[1] For a fuller explanation, see *E.H.S.*, p. 311.

CHAPTER VI

THE DOCTRINE OF SYNONYMOUS CHANGE

Primary Importance of Signification. Originally all names were words, and exactly in the same way that we can express a given statement by more than one combination of words, so formerly the identification of a person by alternative designations, the signification remaining the same, was a common practice calling for no comment.

In the thirteenth century when secondary descriptions were obtaining greater recognition, there being no fewer than six languages spoken in the British Isles, namely English, Welsh, Cornish, Gaelic, Irish and French, besides a little Manx, Norse, and Hebrew, with Latin in common use for legal records, it was further equally correct to describe a man in any one of those languages, and locality and chance were accountable for the form in which his family name ultimately became established. In this manner the number of surnames greatly increased, and yet further variants arrived through corruption, caused by one part of the population not understanding the language or dialect of the other.

Considering a common characteristic description, as Eng. Reade, with its dialectic variants, Ridd, Rudd, we also find as surnames, Rouse (Fr.), Goff (W.), Couch, Ridd (Corn.), Rufus (Lat.), Routh (Scand.), and Rowe

(Ir.). The Gaels also use yellow in the same descriptive sense, giving surnames, Boyd and Buie, and a Welsh thirteenth-century description was Velyn, with the like signification. Another instructive example of the same class is found in the Halesowen Court Rolls, where one family is named Petiwill, Wilkin, and la Lutle.

A common local description, as atte Wood, gave surnames Atwood and Wood, to appear in early official records as de Bosco (Lat.). Some equivalent surnames are Dubois (Fr.), from which came Boyce; Coat and Goss (Corn.); Kelly (W. and Corn.); Kelt (Gael. *coillte*, 'woods'), and possibly Colley (Gael. *coille*). Of the genealogical class may be instanced Sweetlove from the Teutonic personal name Swetleof, and its equivalent Douceamour.

Occupational names likewise provide synonyms. An Israelite bearing the name Cohen might be alternatively described as Episcopus (Lat.), l'Eveske (Fr.), or Bishop (Eng.). The ubiquitous Smith has given Faber (Lat.), Angove (Corn.), Gow (Gael.), a thirteenth-century Welsh equivalent being Egof, the modern Goff, and a possible synonym of French origin is Feaviour (O.F. *fevre*). A bilingual example is: "W. Fabri occidit Will'm le feure", Cumb. 1279 (Ass. R. 131, m. 7).

Gaelic and English synonyms are common, *e.g.* McShane and Johnson, McAimon and Edmundson, Markey (*marcach*, 'horseman') and Rider. So also French and English: Hakepetit and Hakesmal, both found in the West, Pleynamur and Fullalove or Truelove[1] in the East, Graindorge (Lat. Granordei) and Barlicorn in the North, and Vint-deners and Twentipens were interchangeable descriptions of one person in the South.

[1]J. Playnamur dictus Treweloue, Ess. 1360. (K.B. 29, 17, m. 1.)

Translation exemplified. The fact that names such as Barlicorn or Nightingale appear also in French and German, in France and Germany respectively, is sometimes held to point to nickname origin, but actually proves nothing. In every case independent inquiry is necessary, since without some early dated examples it is quite impracticable to suggest the source. Nightingale, for instance, is popularly supposed to have been given to one exceptionally gifted as a singer, but careful search reveals nothing pointing to it ever having been an epithet. The French have the surname Rossignol, the Flemings Nachtergall, and the Germans Nachtigal. In English records numerous thirteenth and fourteenth-century notices may be seen.

— Rossinnoil, c. 1203. (Norm. Exch. R.)
Master Pet. Russinol, precentor of York, 1214. (Cl. R.)
Garsya Russinel, alien, 1220. (Cl. R.)
Ralph Russinol, Beds. 1227. (Ass. R. 2, m. 3.)
Rob. Nihtingale, Beds. 1227. (Ass. R. 2, m. 2.)
Master Pet. Rusciniol, 1231. (Papal Reg.)
Boniface Russinol, 1240. (Lib. R.)
Pet. Rossingnol or Russinol, Oxf. 1249–53. (Cl. R.)
W. Russinol, alien, 1255. (Pat. R.)
Cicely Nitinghale, Northants. 1273. (Cl. R.)
Ralph Niktegale, Norf. 1275. (Hund. R.)
Rob. Nitingal, Norf. 1275. (Hund. R.)
W. Russhinol, Northants. 1275. (Ass. R. 1217, m. 34.)
Nich. Nichtegale or Nigtegale, Warw. 1276. (Cl. R.; Ass. R. 1237, m. 24d.)
Alan Nictegale, Lancs. 1279. (Cl. R.)
W. Nythyngal, Northants. 1280. (Ass. R. 1350, m. 69.)
J. Nittegale, Suff. 1288. (K.B.27, 112, m. 23.)
Ph. Nightgale, Heref. 1292. (Pat. R.)
Jehan Rousignol, Paris, 1292. (T.P.)
Hen. Nhytyngale, Oxf. 1294. (G.D.95, m. 10.)
Rob. Nictyngale, Suss. 1296. (Subs. R.)
Thom. Nichtegale, Ess. 1292. (Ass. R. 1311, m. 55.)

Ric. Nightegale, Lincs. 1300. (Pat. R.)
Ph. Nithyngale, Staffs. 1315. (Cl. R.)
Geof. Nightingall, Northants. 1317. (Ass. R. 1366, m. 54.)

Later variants are Nythingale, Suff. 1327; Nittynggale, Suff. 1327; Nytyhol, Suff. 1334; Nyghtynghale, Surr. 1329; Nethengale, Ess. 1330; Nutegale, Suss. 1332; Nyttynggale, Derb. 1332; Nightegale, Notts. 1336; Nightyngale or Nightegale, Bucks. 1337; and Nightgale, Yorks. 1348, practically every notice providing a new spelling.

The impression gained by consideration of these examples is that the surname was an alien importation, accepted in the form Russinol. On the assumption that the name had the meaning of *rossignol* it was changed to Nightingale, as the Bedfordshire and Northamptonshire items illustrate. Alternative suggestions may be made; for instance, the numerous fourteenth-century occurrences in East Anglia, and the south-east point to the possibility of a Flemish source, but the origin may be indigenous. According to Wheatley, Nightingale Lane in East Smithfield is derived from Cnihtena Guild Lane, providing an excellent illustration of the corruption to be expected in the surname. Nightingale is a village in Wales, two places in the North of France are called Rossignol, and there was Russingnole, perhaps in Italy[1] (1280, Cl. R.) The possibilities for local origin are great; in England, for instance, Nightingale might be Nithinghall or *healh* (cf. Nidingworth, Hunts. Ass. R. 1228, m. 7.) and more than one locality may have been so named. Repinghale of the Hundred Rolls, 1275, has become Rippingale; Whytenhall, 1356, was also written Whitingale (cf. Hugh Kylyngall or Kelynghall, Durh., 1509;

[1] Cf. Chantemerle, Chantecoq, Chanteloup, common place-names in France.

Pard. R.). Nothing whatever points to the name ever having been a nickname here or in France, and just as it is, in some cases, a translation in England, so it may be in Flanders or Germany.

Suppositional Synonyms. Not only were the changes rung on actual synonyms, but also, through misunderstanding resulting from ignorance of the true meaning, as in the case of Nightingale, by what may be termed suppositional synonyms. Other examples are Cavendish, which sounding like 'giving dish' to the Manxman, became Corjeag; Birmingham, for no very clear reason, being turned into Magorisk in Ireland.

Many absurdities on the early rolls are due to the official clerk's practice of rendering English and French names into Latin, which custom prevailed for over two hundred years after the Conquest:—thus Herring from the Teut. Hæring, being popularly supposed to be a nickname from the fish, was accordingly latinised Halec or Alec; Lilburn, a local surname from several counties, on the supposition of it being L'Isle-burn, was turned into De Insula Fontis; Horn, an O.E. personal name, being entered on the rolls, as Cornutus, *i.e.* 'horned'; and a similar process made the name God or Gode, thought to be 'good', into Bon; thus Richard the knave of Gode or Bon occurs both as Richard Godknave and Richard Bonknave in a Leicestershire roll of 1247 (Ass. R. 455, m. 12).

True Synonyms. Translation having been so generally practised, it will be accepted that a change over from one word to another of the same language, the signification remaining practically the same, became commonplace. As proof of this most important feature the following examples are particularly satisfying:

Gaufridus Bursaria is also described as Monetarius, 1159 (Pipe R.)

Peter le Chapman, Suff. 1305 (Ass. R. 843, m. 23.) The same person is Peter le Marchaunt, Suff. 1306 (Ass. R. 845, m. 5.)

Ric. le Charpentir, in Eccleshale, Staffs. 1327, occurs as Ric. le Wryth in the same place, 1332. (Subs. Salt O.S. vii, 211, and x, 96.)

Adam le Corviser, in Bettileye, Staffs. 1327, occurs as Adam le Souter in the same place, 1332. (Subs. Salt O.S. cii, 207, and x. 101.)

Henr. le Drovere in Wyston, Staffs. 1327, occurs as Henr. le Carter in the same place, 1333. (Subs. Salt O.S. vii, 238, and x, 122.)

J. Hunte alias Slaughtyrladde, Soms. 1346. (K.B.9, 229, no. 187.)

Rog. Cristemasse alias Yool, Lond. 1386. (Pat. R.)

David Peyntour alias dictus Steynour. 1403? (K.B.9, 46, m.5.)

Henr' Webstere p' nomen Henr' Wever de Bury s'c'i Ed'i, wever, Suff. 1425. (G.D. 206, m. 8.)

Joh'es Joynour alias dictus Joh'es Carpenter, Midx. 1432. (K.B.29, 91, Hil. 10 Hen. 6.)

Hugo Harper de Wolpet, tregettour, alias d'cus Hugo Mynstrall de Bildeston, jogelour, Suff. 1438. (G.D.210, m. 13d.)

Thomas Schawer de villa de Halesworth alias dictus Thomas Barber, husbandman, 15th cent. (Schawer is an obsolete form of shaver). *E.H.S.*, p. 195.

Rob'tus Smyth alias dictus Rob'tus Lorymer (*i.e.* bit-maker) alias dictus Rob'tus Marchall (*i.e.* shoeing-smith), Surr. 1495. (K.B. 29, 136, Mich. 11 Hen. 7.)

Edw. Doucheman alias dictus Edw. Frise, Surr. 1509. (K.B.29,. 142, m. 22d.)

J. Parker alias Keper, Suss. 1561. (Ass. 35, 3.)

The change sometimes was partial only:—

Geof. Smerekeruere or Smeremonger, Ess. 1327. (G.D. 18a, mm. 9, 10.)

W. Hangethef or Hangedogge, Suff. 1349. (S.C.2, 204/3, mm. 9, 10.)

Geo. Greneland alias dictus Geo. Grenefeld, Surr. 1460. (K.B.29, 91, Hil. 38 Hen. 6.)

Joh'es Goodbody alias dictus Goodman, Norf. 1468. (G D. 207, m.5.)

Rob. Brewer or Brewster or Breuwarne, Leic. 1509. (Pard. R.)

Nich. Oxenherd or Oxenman, Lincs. 1509. (Pard. R.)

These examples cover all four classes of surnames, the

true synonyms being entirely occupational. More rarely the change might be from one class to another, thus Ralph le Cornwaleys, 1292 (Ass. R. 136, m. 10d.) is the same person as Ralph de Cornubia, 1292 (Ass. R. 985, m. 6), and he is first called by a characteristic and secondly by a local name, both practically conveying the same description.

That the practice of synonymous change continued until the seventeenth century may be gathered from Ben Jonson (*Bartholomew Fayre*, 1614, iv, 4), who makes Waspe say: "Why, Mistress, I knew Adam the Clerke, your husband, when he was Adam Scrivener, and writ for two pence a sheet." Here, of course, the synonym is not perfect, Clerk being considered a superior vocation to Scrivener.

Origin of Shakespeare. Resulting from the belief that the signification of a name had greater value than its orthography, it became possible for members of one family, not only to adopt different names with the same meaning, but also by misunderstanding to acquire surnames neither orthographically nor semantically the same. Failure to realise the prevalence of the practice and the errors proceeding therefrom, has resulted in the nature of many surnames being mistaken, and the widespread but erroneous belief that so many appellatives, although actually of local and genealogical origin, perpetuate medieval nicknames.

Of misunderstood surnames no one is of greater fame than that of Shakespere (now Shakespeare), a designation found in most of the counties of England, but yet, notwithstanding extensive research, can boast no great antiquity, being unknown earlier than the fourteenth century, except for one example in Surrey (1268), and a possible entry as Sakespere (Glouc. 1248) that may be on a par with Shakespere (Kent 1279), a clerical changeling as explained below.

Owing to the early families of Shakespere being of no great standing, and the consequent few entries regarding them on the rolls, it has not been possible to obtain a direct statement bearing on the origin of the name, but the available evidence pieced together points to it having arisen in various distinct ways in different parts of the country. Making all allowance for the relative preservation of thirteenth and fourteenth-century records, and comparing the wide-spread instances drawn from Youghal to Kent, in documents of the latter period, with its almost entire absence in those of the thirteenth, it has to be concluded that the historic appellative must have been derived from some other name understood, rightly or wrongly, to have the same signification. No deduction can be made from the Gloucestershire example, but in Kent, of momentary existence, it was a mistake for Shakespey, doubtless a variant of Saxby, an established surname of the county, and the Surrey instance will be noticed shortly as an example of the doctrine of synonymous change.

Of the probable sources of Shakespere, one name is Brekespere, the origin of which has not yet been determined, but is said to have been a locality near Harefield, Uxbridge, Midx.[1] Adrian IV (1154), the only Englishman who ever occupied the papal chair, born near Harefield, c. 1100, was described by the name Brekespere, said to have been changed on the Continent to the supposed equivalent Bricelaunce (Hastafragus in Latin documents). The remotest occurrence of the English form of the name now to be traced is in a

[1] The only reference now existing, seems to be a lease dated 1371, which names 'William Brekespere of Brekespere'. A. H. Tarleton, in *Nicholas Breakspear*, 1896, p. 16.

Buckinghamshire feodary of the year 1166. For that county early documentary evidence is scarce, and, except for an entry in 1286, nothing more of Brekespere has been noticed, and not until 1499 does Shakespere appear. No connection between the two names has been noticed, but conclusive evidence that they were interchangeable is provided by the entry in the Bishop of London's register (1513)—"Saunders alias Breakspear alias Shakspeeres"—no county being stated.[1] The excuse for the substitution is not far to seek. A spear, except for the head, was merely a shaft of timber, and 'to shak', when speaking of wood, signified to 'split' or 'crack', so that disregarding any original meaning of the name, doubtless, by that time forgotten, *shake spere* was a perfectly reasonable interchange with *breke spere.* That in some counties Shakespere became established as a supposed equivalent of Brekespere cannot be doubted, and the following additional examples support this view.

Surrey.	Geof. Brekespere, Brixton Hd. 1206, 1207. (Cur. Reg. R.)
	Geof. Shakespere, Brixton Hd. 1268. (J.W. Ryland.)
Dublin.	Walt. Brekespere, 1285. (Cal. of Docts., Ireland.)
	Thom. Brekespere, 1299. (Irish Just. R.)
	Ric. Shakespere, 1305. (*Ibid.*)
	Rog. Brekspere, 1306. (*Ibid.*)

In Warwickshire, the renowned Shakespere's county, the name Brekespere has not been traced, nor are any ancient references to Shakespere known, the earliest dated instance found by the writer, occurring in Coventry for the year 1358, and while the first of the name may have been an incomer, the possibility exists that here again occurs the synonymous change. Much older names in Coventry were Scathelok and Shakelok, equivalents as will be illustrated below, both doubtless

[1] *E.H.S.*, p. 312.

being derived from the same O.E. personal name, *sceaft* and *loc* being suitable elements. The fourteenth-century difference between Shakelok and Shakespere is not great; 'to spar or sperre' formerly signified 'to lock or bolt', and a *sperel* was a bolt. (cf. Drawelok and Drawespere, Godlok and Godspere.) It is therefore suggested that a practicable origin of Shakespere in Warwickshire is Shakelok otherwise Scathelok.

So far as the possibility of characteristic and occupational source or derivation of the name Shakespere is concerned reference may be made to the full discussion in the *History of Surnames*. Not the slightest evidence is forthcoming to support the popular belief that Shakespere ever figured as a characteristic description or nickname. Doubtless many of the other surnames of similar type which, from appearance only, past writers have supposed to perpetuate ancient nicknames, have nothing whatever to do with personal habits, and given sufficient examples, would be discovered to be changelings from more reasonable names. The student would be well advised to give this phase of onomatology earnest attention, it being of absorbing interest, but he must have patience.

Synonymous Elements. Some actual examples of the use of synonymous elements will be found of interest. Lance, staff, shaft, haft, spere, and baston, being formerly precise equivalents, led to a crop of synonymous surnames. Stakes or poles were also used in similar manner to spears in defence against horsemen. Break might also be written Bruse or Brise (Fr.).

Lincoln.	Alex. Brekespere, c. 1200. (Cur. Reg. R.)
	Rob. Bruselaunce, 1275. (Hund. R.)
	Rob. Brekestaf, 1339. (Pat. R.)
Oxford.	Reg. Waggebastun, 1228. (Cl. R.)
	Walt. Waggestaf, 1275. (Hund. R.)

Norfolk. Rob. Waggespere, 1306. (Cl. R.)
Hen. Waggestaf, 1389. (Pat. R.)

Northants. Nich. Bricelaunce, Edw. I. (Abb. Plac.)
Hen. Shakelaunce, 1275. (Hund. R.)

Lincoln. Thom. Waggespere, 1303. (Ass. R. 1327, m. 25d.)
Rog. Waggestaft, 1317. (Cl. R.)

Gloucester. J. Bruselaunce, mayor, 1229. (Hist. of Bristol, W. Barrett, p. 699.)
W. B(r)ekspere, 1303. (Ass. R. 1327, m. 2d.)
Rob. Brekedaunce (*sic*), 1332. (Pat. R.)

The same family:—

Balsall. J. Shakehaft, 1520. (Rental & Survey, Aug. Off.361, f.13.)
J. Shakstafe, 1520. (Subs. 192/139, m. 3d.)
J. Shakeshafte, 1543. (Subs. 192/156, m. 38.)

The same person:—

Coventry. Sim. and Thom. Skakelock or Schakelock, 1285. (Ass. R. 956, m. 46.)
Nich. Skatheloc, 1363. (Ass. R. 1467, m. 15d.)
Nich. Shakelok, 1364. (Ass. R. 1482, m. 5.)
W. Shakelok, 1372. (Ass. R. 1482, m. 5.)
W. Scathelok, 1381. (Ass. R. 1488, mm. 30, 53, 68d.)
Alan Schaclok or Scathelok, 1411. (Coventry Rental, mm. 103b, 194b.)

Essex. Ric. Scathelok, 1312. (Pat. R. p. 531.)
Ric. Shakelok, 1312. (*Ibid.*)

Herts. Rob. Longstaf, 1333. (G.D.22, m. 13d.)
Rob. Longestak, 1333. (G.D.22, m. 13d.)

Snitterfield. Ric. Shakstaff, 1533. (Warw. Coll. R.)
(Warw.) Ric. Shakespere, 1535. (*Ibid.*)

Freinden. J. Sakespey, 1279. (Ass. R. 369, m. 1.)
(Kent) J. Shakespere, 1279. (Ass. R. 371, m. 1.)
Cf. $y=r$ in Pyghaye and Pyggehare, Suff. 1276. (Ass. R. 1228, m. 6.)

Tockwith. Ric. de Saxby, c. 1285. (Chart. R., 4 Edw. 2.)
(Yorks.) Ric. Shakespey, 1292. (Cott. MS. Vesp. A iv, f. 146.)

While any one set of these examples taken by itself

may not be very impressive, collectively they have more weight, and substantiate the view that numbers of our curious surnames, popularly believed to be nicknames, are nothing more than supposed synonyms of some more ancient appellative.

So important is the doctrine of synonymous change that it may be emphasised further by a pedigree of the *name* of Shakespere of counties Warwick and Gloucester, which although *partly conjectural*, illustrates at a glance the nature of the processes operating towards the multiplication of surnames.

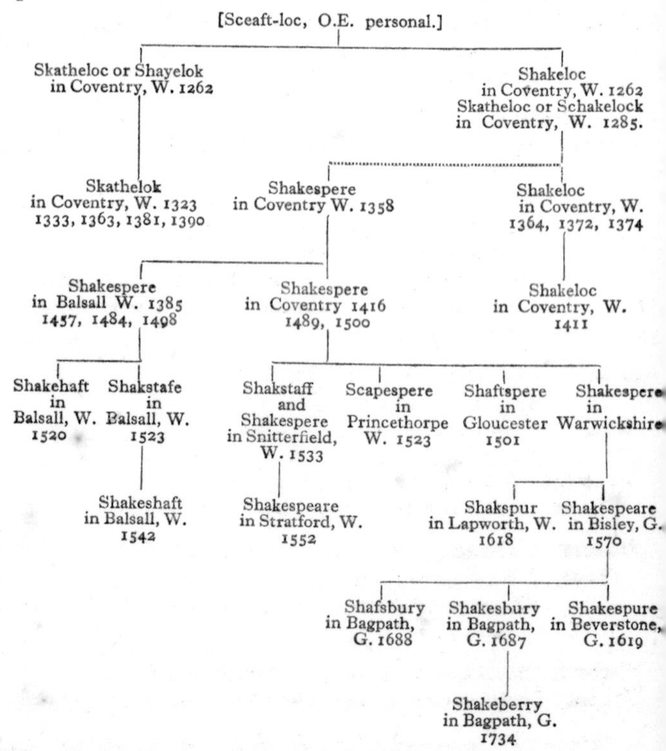

It will be seen that a conjectural O.E. personal name Sceaftloc (known elements being *sceaft*, 'shaft', and *loc* and *lac*, with numerous significations),[1] after several centuries, becomes both Scatheloc and Shakeloc, surnames proved to be interchangeable by several definite entries in the public records. In the thirteenth century this family and in the fourteenth that of Shakespere, both of Coventry, were in very poor circumstances, the Shakeloks being paupers, and a Shakespere worth but 2*s*., consequently little information concerning them is obtainable. It is not surprising, therefore, that no direct statement connecting one name with the other has come to hand, and the argument which has to be adopted is that Shakelok being synonymous with Shakespere, a change over from one to the other was as probable as in many of the known cases instanced above. All three appellatives continued for some time in Coventry, from which City the name, in various forms, spread throughout the counties of Warwick and Gloucester, often shooting off yet further variants as far from the norm as Shakeberry. In other counties, as noticed above, Shakespeare may be derived from Brekespere, and in others again from Saxby.

[1] 'Scaftleich' occurs in the 8th cent. codex of Lorsch Abbey, Germany (n. 467).

CHAPTER VII

CHARACTERISTIC DESCRIPTIONS AND SURNAMES

A Complete System of Surnames. The following classification has been adopted.

	Group I. Inherited Surnames	*Page* 99
	Class. I. *Characteristic Surnames*	
(*A*)	From Appearance.	100
(*B*)	From Character, *i.e.* mental and moral attribute or peculiarity.	104
(*C*)	From Physical Attribute.	106
(*D*)	From Possession.	107
(*E*)	From Action or Habit.	107
(*F*)	From Condition or Quality.	111
(*G*)	From Relationship, *i.e.* consanguinity, kinship.	111
(*H*)	From Race or Sept.	112
	Class II. *Local Surnames*	
(*A*)	From Place of Residence or Work.	117
(*B*)	From Late Place of Residence.	125
	Class III. *Genealogical Surnames*	
(*A*)	From Personal Name of Male Parent.	133
(*B*)	From Personal Name of Female Parent.	137
(*C*)	From Personal Name of other Relative.	138
(*D*)	From Description or Surname.	139
	Class IV. *Occupational Surnames*	
(*A*)	From Office or Profession.	147
(*B*)	From Mock Office.	148
(*C*)	From Military Rank.	149
(*D*)	From Trade or Vocation.	150

Group I (Inherited Surnames). Class I. Of the four classes in group I, that of characteristic surnames is of the most varied nature and, consequently of greatest interest. The personal description was one of the most ancient methods of indicating the individual, and in the days before second-names became hereditary, those describing some peculiarity of the bearer formed the largest category, but with the growth in the more convenient use of addresses and occupations as distinctions, the characteristic has become the smallest class of surnames, amounting to from 6 to 10 per cent. Reference may be made to page 22 for examples of the O.E., Welsh, and Irish characteristic descriptions in use long before the second-name had obtained the permanency and sharing nature of the family name. The bearer of an authenticated name of this class has a very good clue to the most prominent feature of an ancestor flourishing at the time when surnames were acquiring an hereditary nature. What was his peculiarity? The answer may be in one of several languages, and it may be a noun, as Lombard; an adjective, as White; an adjective + noun, as

Longsmith; or possibly a verb + noun, but such names are usually either temporary nicknames as Findesilver; or describe work, as Catchpole or Copestake, and so are more properly classified as occupational.

Although there are a great number of surnames which appear to fall into this category, and are, in fact, so placed by the superficial etymologist, yet upon a searching investigation comparatively few pass the test. Names like Bidgood, Blythman, Bunting, Dearlove, Drinker (occ.), Giddy, Licorice, Peacock, Puttock, Quick (loc.), Rigmaiden (loc.), Seafoul, Smallman, Smart, Stout (loc.), Sweatinbed, Toogood, and Vigorous, have all been cited by earlier writers as nicknames, that is, of the characteristic class, whereas not one actually comes into that division. All are genealogical, except those marked otherwise, and examples, chronologically arranged, forming the proof, may be seen in the *History of Surnames* (pp. 337–44).

Before a name can be classified or its original significance determined, localised and dated occurrences should be obtained, when the true nature may perhaps be discovered, as has been done in the case of Nightingale (see above, p. 87), and Metcalf (p. 73).

(I.*A*) **Surnames from Appearance.** The examples already given have demonstrated that a description of the personal appearance among Celtic and Gothic races was a favourite method of distinguishing one man from another, but it is rather surprising to find how few epithets of that nature have survived as surnames, pointing perhaps to the distinctions in appearance having been individual, and not passed on to the succeeding generations sufficiently often to become established as family names. In the earlier official records French and Latin descriptions are principally found, English examples becoming more noticeable in the fourteenth century. References to hirsuteness were frequent:—

Ælfsige mid tham berde, Dev. 11th. c. (Thorpe, p. 640.)
Rob. cum barba, Bucks. 1247. (Ass. R. 56, m. 13d.)
Rob. ove la Barbe, Bucks. 1286. (Cl. R.)
W. with the berde, Bucks. 1315. (Ass. R. 70, m. 2d.)
W. Wyththeberd, Bucks. 1315. (Ass. R. 70, mm. 3d. 71.)

Confusion with Whitebeard and Whitbread seems inevitable, possibly they are all of the same origin. The 'Bearded Lady' is represented by Alice Barbe Dor, Northants, 1247 (Ass. R. 56, 25d.), and a much admired man must have been Hugh Belebarb, Midx. 1205. (Cur. Reg. R.). Jews, never considerately treated, often had uncomplimentary labels thrust upon them, but 'Moses cum naso' received full recognition for his prominence! Another Israelite was 'Deudone cum pedibus tortis' (with the crooked feet), a Norman being dubbed Tortesmains (twisted hands). In the same way most parts of the body were noticed, but few of the epithets ever became hereditary family names, and their use is illustrative of the scarcity of real surnames.

It is not easy to obtain evidence of the origin of names of this subclass, and some inquirers dispose of the difficulty by declaring that none is required for what is obvious, but as exemplified above, surnames which, hitherto, have been looked upon as deriving from personal epithets are, upon examination, somewhat disconcertingly discovered to be something quite different. Even the very commonest of characteristic descriptions, as White, Brown, or Black, may be and often are derived from baptismal names. Blac, Hwita, Brun, and also Pinca and Grene, were undoubtedly O.E. personal appellatives.

Blac, Suss. Yorks. 1086. (Dom. Bk.); also Blacsune (Dom. Bk.)
Whita, Suff. 1086. (Dom. Bk.)
Sewine Pinca, 11th cent. (Thorpe, 632.)
Rob. fil' Bruni, Norf. 1166. (Pipe R.); also Brunesune (Dom. Bk.)
Adam Pink, Norf. 1275. (Hund. R.); As an apocope, see above, p. 60.
Pynkesymond de Charleton, Berks. 1294. (G.D.96, m. 5.)
Godwin Grenessone, Hants. 1103–15. (Liber Winton.)

But what of Blue, Yellow, Grey, Blund, and Read (Red), all modern surnames? They cannot be traced as font-names, but in Domesday Book may be seen as a personal name, Bloiet, presumably the origin of Blewett, Bluett, etc. popularly supposed to be nick-names. Blue may also have been of local origin (Joldewin de Blue, 1226. Cl. R.); from Blois in France. Le Bloy also occurs twice in 1216–8 (Cl. R.), Bardsley making the entries into le Bleu, evidence of a nickname origin! The article is doubtless a clerical error for the preposition. Gilbert le Yelewe, occurs in a Herefordshire roll, 1256 (Ass. R. 300c, m. 24). Grey is also to be found with the article, but seems to be a local description of early date, *e.g.* Anchitil de Grai, Oxf. 1086 (Dom. Bk.); Rob. de Gray, Oxf. 1275 (Hund. R.). Blund and Read have the appearance of genuine characteristic surnames, the latter being found in several languages (see above p. 85). Owing to its early popularity as a font-name, Brown, in modern directories, occupies far more space than Black, Read, and others.

The fact that some of these very simple names are clearly derived from more than one source shows the necessity for taking extreme care, and in no case should a final decision be made without evidence. A short selection of modern surnames may be of interest.[1]

[1] *E.H.S.*, p. 224.

English: Ballard (bald-headed), Blackbeard, Fairfax (fair hair), Little. *French:* Bass (*le bas*, 'the low' *i.e.* 'small'), Chaff (*le chauvre*, 'the bald'), Grose (*le gros*, 'the fat'); Diminutives:—Basset (dwarf), Blundell (blonde), Russell (red). *Latin:* Rufus (red). *Welsh:* Cloff (lame), Goran (dwarf), Lloyd (*llwyd*, 'grey'), Vaughan (*bychan*, 'little'), Wynne (*gwyn*, 'fair'). *Cornish:* Angwin (the white), Coad (old), Couch (red), Vian, Veen (little). *Gaelic:* Dunn (brown), Campbell (*cam beul*, 'wry mouthed'), Muir (*mor*, 'great'). *Scottish:* Lang, Laing. *Irish:* Bawn (*bán*, 'white'), Begg (*beag*, 'little'), Crone (*crôn*, 'brown'), Duff (*dubh*, 'black'), Glass (*glas*, 'grey'), Woney (*uaitne*, 'green'). *Scandinavian:* Routh (*hrutr*, 'red'). *Alien:* Schwartz (black), Weiss (white).

Very popular were descriptions of limbs, even King Edward I, who had remarkably long legs, became known as Longshanks. Well-known surnames are Cruikshanks (Scot.), Sheepshank, Foljambe, other descriptions which had passing popularity being:—

Geoff. Blacschonke, Dev. 1272. (Ass. R. 1230, m. 59d.)
Gilb. Greyschanke, Cambs. 1275. (Hund. R.)
Alex. Belejambe, Shrops. 1275. (Hund. R.)
Adam Brunshonk, Lincs. 1276. (Ass. R. 1222, m. 15d.)
G. Langeshank, Scot. 1306. (Ir. Just. R.)
Ric. Limelesse, Yorks. 1333. (G.D. 123, m. 26.)
J. Bareshanke, Northants. 1333. (G.D. 123, m. 20.)
J. Shortshank, Yorks. 1379. (Poll Tax, p. 54.)
Ric. Qwytschank, Yorks. 1379. (Poll Tax, vii, 167.)
Marg. Smaleshankes, Lond. 1573. (St. Michael, Cornhill Reg.)

Possibly also may be included:—

Gilb. Foleshanke, Rutl. 1299. (Ass. R. 728, m. 2d.). Cf. Foulschanck.

Ralph Caponleg, Yorks. 1361. (G.D. 145, m. 11d.)

J. Philipschank, Yorks. 1379. (Poll Tax, p. 104.) *i.e.* sparrow-legged.

Ric. Craneshanke, Ess. 1412. (C.P. 40, 607, m. 70.)

The Welsh had Bongam and Vongam (the crookedshanked), and Libin (a lank one); the Flemings, Waghenbeen (*waeghe been*, 'unsteady leg'); and the Northmen, Fôtr (limp leg).

Names comprising epithet + personal name, as Meiklejohn (Big John), or epithet + trade, as Micklewright, also appear.

Shorthobbe de Weston, Bucks. 1328. (Ass. R. 75, m. 5d.)
Ric. Longaleyn, Suff. 1358. (G.D. 139, m. 18.)
J. Shortrobynson, Beds. 1403. (G.D.190, m. 1d.)
J. Liteljohn, Dev. c. 1417. (E370, 3/20.)
J. Smalehobbe, Herts. 1418. (K.B.9, 212, no. 67.)

Thom. le Langependere, Cumb. 1278. (Ass. R. 133, m. 21.)
Hug. fil' Longifabri, Berks. 1295. (G.D.96, m. 13.)
W. Longeclerk, Berks. 1296. (G.D.96, m. 32.)
J. Littelsmyth, Northumb. 1339. (G.D. 132, m. 13.)

Smaleman and Lytelman were O.E. personal names, but Lytelboy may be derived from a locality (Lillebois) as was Tallboy (*taille bois*, 'cut wood'), if it be not Litelbodi (cf. Godeboy and Godebodi). Alice Longynough was a nun of Amesbury, 1399 (K.B. 9, 183, no. 27), and doubtless derived her name from some longen-hough, 'long hill', cf. Birchenough.

J. Litelbodi, Bucks. 1261. (Ass. R. 58, m. 20d.)
J. Lytelboy, Bucks. 1389. (G.D. 14, m. 18d.)

The thorough investigator will find that surnames which, without doubt, can be assigned to this subclass (appearance) are few, and numbers that at a first glance might be so placed, are found upon examination to be of entirely different nature, such as Sheepshead (loc.), Blackbrow (loc.), Whalebelly (Whaleborough?), Fairman (gen.), Thornback (loc.), etc.

(I.*B*) **Surnames from Character.** The natures of

persons or particular traits have always served as descriptions, *e.g.* Alfred the Great, Philip the Cruel, and so on. The distinctions which appear to fall into this subclass are seldom traceable as surnames.

— Fairandgode, Yorks. 1337. (Chanc. Inq., no. 1487.)
Pet. Richeandgood, Kent. 1372. (E179, 123/29, m. 40.)
Ric. Scatergood, Derby. 1549. (Pat. R.)

Scattergood, which occurs in the Hundred Rolls (1275), as Schatregod, was evidently a personal name, and probably the others are corruptions in like manner. In some cases like that of the Yorkshire felon, Hugh Proud of Noght, the curious description is perhaps nothing more than a combination of the surname Proud and a place-name such as Nutt. Proud itself may fall into this subclass, but it is more probably a survival of the Anglo-Saxon baptismal name Prud.

Rob. le Simple, Midx. 1202. (Cur. Reg.)
Syward le Wise, Bucks. 1247. (Ass. R. 56, m. 16d.)
Margery la Sage, Northants. 1247. (Ass. R. 56, m. 24d.)
Hugh le Noble, Bucks. 1247. (Ass. R. 56, m. 36.)
W. le Megre, Bucks. 1286. (Ass. R. 65, m. 20.)
Ph. le Large, Dors. 1299. (G.D. 98, m. 5.)

It is by no means certain that even these simple names are what they appear to be, for instance Noble may be from the personal name. (cf. Edwi Nobol, Dev. 11th c., Thorpe, p. 636; J. Nobilson, Lincs. 1451; K.B. 29, 91, Hil. 29 Hen. 6.) Bardsley pointed out that in the Hundred Rolls (1275) eight persons out of nine called le Wise resided either in Oxfordshire or Cambridgeshire, adding "no doubt all were University men". Perhaps the Canon joked, for actually it is to be noted that the bearers of the label of intellectuality were nearly all 'clod-hoppers' of varying degree, villains, cottars, and natives! Other possibilities may be suggested by the following entries:—

"Will's le Vyse de Vyse," Wilts. 1441. (K.B. 29, 91, Mich. 20 Hen. 6.)

Sim. Fitz or Vice, Beds. 1509. (Pard. R.)

No doubt "Shakespeare" chose the name Shallow for his country justice, as he did Silence and Slender, for its appropriateness, and without any knowledge of it being a real surname, yet it is quite possible that he had run across it, Shallow (inaccurately called le Shallowe), a Frenchman, becoming naturalised, having settled down in Aldersgate Ward. In various later records his name occurs Shallowe (1567), Shallo (1568), Shalwaye (1571), and Shalloway (1576), the Englishman's spelling of one or other of the French surnames Chaillot, Chaillou or Chailloux, which are evidently derived from such place-names as Chalaux, Chalou, Chaillot, Chaillou, or Chailloué, the last being particularly like Shalloway. It is of interest to note further that, as early as 1284, Chayllou appears in a Cornish Assize Roll, and by 1327, Chaillo, Chaillou, and Challou occur in the Subsidy Rolls of Devonshire, where so many Frenchmen established themselves. Shallow, in some cases, is an Irish name, from Ó Sealdhaigh.

(I.*C*) **Surnames from Physical Attribute.** In the days when a dispute in the legal courts might be judicially settled by the result of a duel between the litigants, and right was to a large extent subjected to might, very great notice was taken of powerful physique, and the capacity to fight. Who has not heard of Richard, dubbed Cœur-de-lion, in recognition of his gallant exploits? A few descriptions of this nature have survived, as

Armstrong, Lauder (Ir. *laidir* 'strong'), and Fort (Fr. strong). Firebrace and Fairbrass, occurring as Ferebrache in 1190 (Pipe R.), are forms of a name of Norman origin, signifying 'iron-arm'. Dent-de-fer, 1230, is of similar type, and may be rendered Strong-tooth (Pipe R.). Strongman (Scot. Strangman,) like Smallman, may have been originally an O.E. font-name. Vigorous, which occurs also as Vigrass, was a Norman personal name.

(I.*D*) **Surnames from Possession.** Descriptions may refer to property or the want of it, a typical royal epithet of this subclass being Sansterre or Lackland, applied to John, youngest son of Henry II, because he held no fief under his father. Of the few surnames may be noticed Sanzaver (*sans avoir*, 'without property'), which was latinised *sine Averio* (1201, Cur. Reg. R.). Shorthose is another possible example, as is Poingdestre, from the heraldic charge.

Simon the hors, Ess. 1282. (Ass. R. 1255, mm. 4, 15.)
Rog. cum le Bell, Suff. 1282. (K.B. 27, 71, m. 6.)
W. Withegynnes, Notts. 1302. (K.B. 27, 168, m. 43.)
Thom. Grenekyrtel, Leic. 1308. (Borough Rec. i, 373). But cf. Grimkettle.
Nich. Withthesherte, Suff. 1315. (K.B. 27, 222, m. 112.)
Ric. cum Equo (with the horse), Hunts. 1327. (Subs.)
W. Blakmantel, Chesh. 1334. (Chester 29, 45, m. 9.)
J. Whitegown, Scottesman, 1448. (K.B. 29, 91, East. 26 Hen. 6.)

Perhaps of this class was W. Modernaked (*i.e.* stark naked), Warw. 1292 (G.D. 91, m. 12d.), but this curious description may be local like the Sussex Halfnaked.

(I.*E*) **Surnames from Action or Habit.** An exceptional act or a peculiar trait of a person was liable to be used as the distinctive label in the records, or as an identifying description among his fellows, but with few exceptions such epithets do not appear to have survived as surnames. There are, however, a great number of descriptions to be found in early documents which, to the superficial investigator, may appear to belong to this subclass, but upon more careful inquiry turn out to be corruptions of something entirely different. For instance, W. Chopcherie, Warw. 1334 (Ass. R. 1400, m. 121d.) is actually a corruption of Chopchurch (see the example, p. 164). Chirche is indistinguishable in some writings from chirthe, which may occur as chirye (cf. *ye* for *the*), which, together with cherie, is to be seen on the above-cited roll. Other names which doubtless can be as satisfactorily explained are:—

J. Pokepot, Ess. 1327. (E179, 107/13, m. 1d.)
J. Ratellebagge, Ess. 1275. (Hund. R.)
W. Spitfat, Herts. 1286. (Ass. R. 325, m. 10.)
Hen. Tukbacon, Yorks. 1394-5. (Surt. Soc. xcvi, 94.)

Numbers of descriptions as curious will be found in Chapter XII, where they are arranged according to their elements. Generally the bizarre appellative makes only one appearance, but occasionally we find one running through several centuries, when a chance is obtained of determining its status. Let us consider Hopshort, generally held to be a nickname.

Hoppescort, Hants. 1168. (Pipe R.) Cf. O.E. elements Oppa and Scorta.
Ralph Hopechort, Surr. 1220. (K.B. 26, 73, m. 18d.)
Hugh Hoppeshort, Lincs. 1255. (Cl. R.)
J. de Hopposchort, Notts. 1271. (Ass. R. 1217, m. 9.)
W. Hobschort, Cumb. 1300. (G.D. 10a, m. 6d.)
Sarra Hopshort, Lincs. 1310. (Pat. R.)
W. Hopshort, Lincs. 1347. (Ass. R. 1437, m. 22.)
J. Hopshort, Lincs. 1402. (E370, 3/4, m. 1d.)

It will be seen that besides the strong indication of genealogical origin, there is a possibility of derivation from a place-name, in which connection may be considered Hoppescotes or Heppescotes (now Hepscott) a place in Northumberland (1280; Ass. R. 1245, m. 73). There is not the slightest evidence pointing to the name having been derived from any action of the first bearer. In like manner investigation dispels the verb + noun illusion which popularly surrounds such names as Benbow, Breakspeare, Crackshield, Hurlbat, Shakeshaft, Shakespeare, Turnbull, Waghorn, etc. For instance, the interesting name Turnbull can be shown to have little or no qualifications to rank as a characteristic surname, and romantic origin, even in Scotland, is by no means certain. Tournebu in Calvados gave rise to a family appellative, which appeared in Hampshire as early as 1155 (Pipe R.), and by the thirteenth century Turnboel, evidently the same, comes on the scene.[1] King John, in 1216, granted lands in Stepney to Robert Turneboel (Cl. R.), and letters patent for 1240, 1252, and 1256 give a Dover name, as Turnebuel, Turneboll, and Torneboel. Early in the fourteenth century the appellative can be traced in Scotland, where from the nature of the entry, it may be inferred that it was something strange and new.

'Willelmo dicto Turnebule,' Selkirk, c. 1315. (Reg. Mag. Sigilla, p. 6.)

There is nothing to show whether it arrived from England or was indigenous, but early Scottish historians, somewhat noted for picturesque inexactitude, claim that the distinction was bestowed by Robert the Bruce upon

[1] In France, where Turnbull is an armigerous family, there are numbers of local names ending in *boeuf*, as Criqueboeuf, Quilleboeuf, etc.

a local hero who, displaying prodigious strength, curbed the evil intentions of an obstreperous bull.[1] The name was also given to a horse, mentioned in a bequest of a Yorkshire testator in 1358. As a surname, Turnbull is found in Berwick-on-Tweed, 1333 (Chanc. Inq.), in Herts. from 1342 (K.B. 29, 5, m. 31), in Cumberland from 1346 (C.P. 40, 342, m. 249d.), in Norfolk from 1356 (Pat. R.), in Yorkshire from 1374 (G.D. 165a, m. 12d.), and Northumberland from 1377 (Pat. R.). Considerable confusion exists with Trumble, Trimble and Tremble, the two latter of which may be of local origin.

Sometimes a verb + noun compound was used as a trade description, and such is really little removed from an occupational appellative.

Ric. Plauntesoyll, Bucks. 1286. (Ass. R. 65, m. 21.)
W. Cuttepurs, Cumb. 1292. (Ass. R. 135, m. 19.)
Hen. Pykestrawe, Suff. 1346. (C.P. 40, 342, m. 371.)

Some tradesmen were curiously described by the goods they vended rather than by their occupational title, in some cases from the custom of crying wares in the streets, and so, if we consider the words 'cryer of' as being understood, their names evidence 'action or habit', and so fall into this subclass. If, however, it be held that the descriptions are obtained from shop signs, and the unexpressed words are 'vendor of', the appellatives would rank as occupational (See also p. 155).

Rog. Freshaddock, Westm. 1279. (Ass. R. 982, m. 28.)
J. Ruskebasket, Cumb. 1292. (Ass. R. 135, m. 25.)
Maud Lusshefissh, Wilts. 1294. (Cl. R.) Luce?
Hen. Swetemylk, Chesh. 1355. (Chester 17, 4, m. 13.)
W. Smalware, Ess. 1363. (C.P. 25(1), 62, 217.)

[1] Descriptive verse together with an account of the death of this gigantic Scotsman in single combat with an English knight will be found in the *History of Selkirkshire* (T. Craig-Brown), vol. II, p. 333.

(I.*F*) **Surnames from Condition or Quality.** Two persons of the same name led to such distinction, as Senior, Younger, and Elder, which in some cases became amily names. Other descriptions of this subclass are Newman, Bastard, and Outlaw. Scottish examples are Auld and Ogg.

W. Hen Flemyngge, Norf. 1359. (G.D. 139, m. 32.)
Thom. le Hen (W. 'the old'), Staffs. 1375. (D.L. 30, 229/12, m. 6.)
Ric. ye Elder, Yorks. 1379. (Poll Tax, p. 214.)
Edm. Yonger, Yorks. 1379. (Poll Tax, p. 279.)

In some cases Elder is genealogical, in others occupaional. The new man found himself labelled with a number of synonyms.

Ailmer Novus homo, Ess. 1203. (Cur. Reg. R.)
W. le Nouelhomme, Bucks. 1247. (Ass. R. 56, m. 12d.)
Rob. Niweman, Cambs. 1275. (Hund. R.)
Gilb. le Neucum or Neucomen, Lincs. 1275. (Hund. R.)
Ric. Nywecomena, Dev. 1333. (E179, 95/7, m. 12d.)
J. Neughcomen, Cumb. 1339. (G.D. 132, m. 6.)

The modern surname Dives, usually from a placename in France, may also fall into this category.

Edeva Dives (the rich), Suff. 1086. (Dom. Bk.)
Ralph Dives, Suff. 1203. (Cur. Reg. R.)

(I.*G*) **Surnames from Relationship.** A curious feature of nomenclature is that terms denoting consanguinity or affinity have been perpetuated as family names, such as Cousin (Couzens, Cossins, Cussen, etc.); Eam, Eames, Neames (O.E. *eam*, 'uncle'); Muff (*maugh*, 'brother-in-law'); Neave, 'nephew'; Uncle, etc., but they sometimes belie their appearance.

Ric. Fader, Bucks. 1247. (Ass. R. 56, m. 40d.)
Ric. le Fader, Oxf. 1275. (Hund. R.)
E. Filiol (godson), Wilts. 1275. (Hund. R.)
Walt. le Neve, Norf. 1275. (Hund. R.)
Ric. le Cusyn, Bedf. 1275. (Hund. R.)
J. le Uncle, Ess. 1275. (Hund. R.)
W. Godmoder, Cambs. 1275. (Hund. R.)
Ric. Goddesone, Staff. 1327. (Subs. 204.)
Margeria Aunte, Staffs. 1327. (Subs. 245.)
Rob. le Em, Staffs. 1327. (Subs. 245.)
J. le Stepson, Norf. 1377. (G.D. 158, m. 6d.)
Agn. Goddoghter, Yorks. 1379. (Poll Tax, p. 55.)

Fader is a Domesday Book personal name, and may sometimes be the title of a priest. Modhere was also a Teutonic name. Godson is probably a survival of a font-name, as may be Cusin, Brother, etc.

De Willelmo f. Brother, Lincs. 1202. (Ass. R.; Stenton.)
Alfrerus f. Brother, Norf. — (Anc. D., A10538.)
Cf. W. le Brother, Oxf. 1275. (Hund. R.) Broiderer?

A Norman example is Beaufitz or Beavis (*beau-fils*, 'son-in-law'), but Beavis is also a local name from Beauvais (France).

(I.*H*) **Surnames from Race or Sept.** Names of this subclass are among the most easy of identification, yet there are pitfalls. Angwin (the Angevin), Brabner (the Brabancon), Breton, Burdeleys (the Bordelais), Burgoyne (the Burgundian), Cornwallis, English, Fleming, French, Inglis, Irish, Gaskin (the Gascon), Lorraine, Scott, Wallis, etc. seem to be unmistakable, but others present difficulties. Aleman, for instance, may be genealogical or occupational, and German and Jarman were common personal names, the former being also a possible local description from St. Germaine, Cornwall, and moreover, several places besides Germany were called Alemannia. Dane is sometimes a form of Dene, and Dennis is from Dionysius. Gwyddel (W. the Irishman) may alternatively be a local description; Lombard becomes confused with Lambard; Petwin (the Poitevin) is indistinguishable from variants of the personal name Peohtwine (O.E. and also Jewish). Michael Noreseman, Cumb. 1279, at once brings to mind the Scandinavian colonists, but in another entry our Viking is called Mich. Nuricesman (Ass. R. 133, m. 21d.), Norice being the M.E. orthography of 'nurse'. Some other instances may be noticed, illustrating not only the making of surnames, but also exemplifying one way in which the strangers lost their native descriptions.

Walt le Aleman, Yorks. 1200. (Cur. Reg. R.)
Maur. le Angevine, Oxf. 1275. (Hund. R.)
Rog. le Brabazoun, Lond. Edw. II. (Plac. de Q.W.)
W. le Breton, Norf. 1275. (Hund. R.)
Hugh. le Burdeleis, Norf. 1180–1. (Pipe R.)
Pet. le Burguillon, Ess. 1285. (Cl. R.)
Rann. le Deneys, Suff. 1249. (Fines, 1836 ed.)
Rog. Ducheman de Braban, Norf. 1376. (G.D. 158, m. 3.)
Walt. le Fleming, Lincs. 1275. (Hund. R.)
W. Florentyn, Surr. 1268. (Pat. R.)
Rob. Lefranceis, Warw. 1174–5. (Pipe R.)
Ric. le Frese, Suff. 1280. (Pat. R.)
W. Gallicus, Wilts. 1202. (Cur. Reg. R.)
Ph. le Gascoyn, Shrops. 1266. (Fines, 1836 ed.)
W. Lombard, Shrops. 1327. (Subs.)
J. le Loreng, Oxf. 1275. (Hund. R.)
J. the Mor, Beds. 1375. (G.D. 152, m. 56.)
Walt. le Norreys, Bucks. 1247. (Ass. R. 56, m. 47d.)
Pet. le Peytevin, Soms. 1250. (Fines, 1836 ed.)
Emma la Picarde, Kent. 1302. (G.D. 26, m. 7.)
Adam Romanus, Glouc. 1204. (Cur. Reg. R.)
Egg. Saracenus, Norf. c. 1195. (Cur. Reg. R.)
Rob. Turk de London, Kent. 1294. (G.D. 26, m. 3.)
N. Turkeys, Lond. 1294. (G.D. 87, m. 29.)
Ric. Turkeys, Norf. 1468. (G.D. 207, m. 3d.)

Since gipsies are not known to have arrived in England much before the year 1500, this entry is interesting: W. Gypcyen (? Egyptian), Bucks. 1286 (Ass. R. 65, m. 42d). The movements of the native British also resulted in new surnames.

Dav. Anglicus, Lincs. 1200. (Cur. Reg. R.)
Ric. le Cornwaleys, Worc. 1290. (G.D. 89, m. 4.)
Rob. le Engleys, Westm. 1310. (Plac. Abbr.)
Rob. Inglys, Yorks. 1345. (Pat. R.)
Ithel Gwethel, Wales, 1292. (Subs. 242/53.)
Agn. la Irysshe, Glouc. 1291. (G.D. 89, m. 4d.)
Walt. le Escot, Glouc. 1232. (Cl. R.)
Thom. le Walys, Bedf. 1275. (Hund. R.)

Mich. le Northerne, Bucks. 1320. (Ass. R. 72, m. 3.)
J. Bynorth, Bucks. 1353. (G.D. 136, m. 18.)
W. Southeron, Yorks. 1379. (Poll Tax, p. 118.)
Walt. Bysoutherne, Worc. 1292. (G. D. 91, m. 11.)
Hen. le Westerne, Bucks. 1320. (Ass. R. 72, m. 2d.)

In similar manner surnames may be derived from counties, as Cornish, Kentish and Devenish, and from places, as Londonish, Blythman, Chesterman, Penkethman, Quickman (Qwyk or Wyke, Yorks. and elsewhere), Churcher and Grover.

Leowine Lundenisca, Dev. 11th c. (Thorpe, p. 635.)
Hen. Londoneys, Bucks. 1330. (G.D. 123, m. 10.)
Rob. Salkeldman, Cumb. 1366. (G.D. 154, m. 1.)
Hen. Riseberger, Surr. 1461. (Fines.)[1]

It is due to the suffixes *-ish*, *-man*, and *-er*, expressing association and so indicating personal peculiarity, that these derivatives are grouped as characteristic names. Assignment to this subclass is often most uncertain

[1] A later entry is: J. Rysebrigger de Albery, 1497 (Subs. p. 108). W. Risbridger of Albury made his will, 1754. Risbridge in Wonersh being but three miles from Albury the derivation of this established surname appears conclusive.

such appellatives being duplicated by identical genealogical and occupational names. Thus, Bridger and Bridgman may be either characteristic or occupational. Hammer and Waldman are characteristic, and also genealogical from O.E. Hæmheard and Wealdman.

Careful analysis shows that names like Multonman, rather than being of the characteristic class, are much more probably compounds of employer's surname and employee's description, *e.g.* a Tadcaster (Yorks.) entry, 1379 has: W. Dryffeld, W. Dryffelman, Agnes serviens Driffeld. Clearly the last two were both servants of the first-named.

Reverting to race the Irish have Brathnagh (Breatnach, 'the Welshman'), Pléamonn (the Fleming), Spainagh (The Spaniard), and Gall (the foreigner). A number of Scottish surnames are derived from Clan names, as Brodie, Buchanan, Cameron, Colquhoun, Douglas, Drummond, Erskine, Fullerton, Graham, Kerr, Lamont, MacQuarrie, Munro, Ogilvie, Ross, Stewart, Urquhart, etc.[1]

[1] *E.H.S.*, p. 227.

CHAPTER VIII

LOCAL DESCRIPTIONS AND SURNAMES

Group I (Inherited Surnames). Class II. The largest of the four classes in group I, so far as England is concerned, comprises not less than 40 to 50 per cent of surnames, being those derived from place-names and topographical features. According to the census of 1881 there were about 16,000 parishes, townships and places in England, and each of these must have covered a number of localities, fields, buildings, etc., known by distinct names, any one of which might have served to describe a person working or dwelling in or about the same. The possible sources for names of the local class might, therefore, run to a million or so, and thousands of these must be lost to the modern investigator. It is not improbable that numbers of our curious surnames are derived from these forgotten place or field-names, and that if identification were possible, the proportion of surnames of local origin would exceed fifty per cent. Even as it is, we find country, province, county, hundred, town, or village drawn upon, the list ranging through forest, river, and field, down to pool, gate, or gutter, providing an answer to the question,—where is or was he located? In Scotland, the North of England, and Cornwall, the choice lay particularly with towns, villages, and hamlets, southern names much more frequently perpetuating features of lesser prominence. Few surnames of the local class originated in Wales or Ireland, but quite a number can be traced to places in Manche, Calvados, Eure, and Seine Inférieure, the more northern departments of France.

The principal languages of the elements of local surnames, are English, French, Scandinavian, Gaelic, and Cornish, and many ancient dialectical and obsolete words, uncompounded or compounded, may be found, the principal grammatical formations being a single-element noun, as Combe (a valley); noun + noun, as Gatehouse and Kinloch (Gael. *ceann*, 'head'); noun + adjective, as Penarth (Corn. *pen*, 'hill'; *arth*, 'high'); adjective + noun, as Freeland and Sowerby (Norse, *saurr*, 'swampy'; *by*, 'homestead'): preposition + noun, as Bywater; and more complicated compounds, as Bullivant (Corn. *pol y font*, 'the head of the spring'), and Beswetherick (Corn. *bos bither ick*, 'the house by the meadow place'). Reference may be made to p. 25 for examples of the O.E., Welsh and Irish local descriptions in use before the coming of the Normans, and to p. 31 for those current in the rolls for a century after the Conquest.

It has been found convenient to divide local surnames into two subclasses according to (*a*) origin from place of residence or work, and (*b*) late place of residence; but it is necessary in many cases, to determine the full history of a name before definitely assigning a name to either the one or the other division.

(II.*A*) **Surnames from Place of Residence or Work.**[1] This large division includes all surnames derived from descriptions of residences, tenures, or places of work, ranging from the great seigniories down to plots of land or household offices. As will have been

[1] *E.H.S.*, p. 228 *et seq.*

noticed above, all the early distinctions of this subclass had prepositions in their composition, and these in a few instances have been retained in the modern family name, as De Courcy, De la Fosse, De Grey, De Gylpyn, Des Vœux; sometimes blending with the following word, as Achurch, Arwennack (Corn. *ar*, 'upon'; *winick*, 'a marsh'), Dangerfield (of Angerville, Normandy), and Upfill (? upper field).

Territorial Surnames.[1] The powerful Norman barons holding under the Crown in the eleventh and twelfth centuries were distinguished by the names of their principal fiefs, English and French, and these in many cases ultimately became fixed as permanent family names. Well-known appellatives of this type are:—De Arundel, de Beauchamp, de Ferrers, de Mortimer, etc. It by no means follows that everyone who proudly bears a name of this nature has ancestry of wealth and power, in fact, the majority are of but lowly origin, it being customary for those having no worldly interest whatsoever to be described by the place from which they migrated. Such appellatives belong to the second subclass of local surnames, but in order to prove the point, the following most instructive selection of names of tradesmen, taken from *Les Rôles de Taille Parisiens*, 1292–1313, may be given here.

Jehan de Bucy, le charpentier; Gefroi de Chartres, pastoier; Jean de Montmorenci, courraier; Guillaume de la Rivière, bouclier; Jehan du Val, chandelier; Philippe de Gournai, orfèvre; Jehan de Pinqueigni, peintre; Jehannot de Montfort, talemalier; Giles de Montigni, ferpier.

It cannot be doubted that among the hordes of French artisans who settled in England, many bore such names,

[1] *E.H.S.*, p. 229.

giving us perhaps some instances of Bussey, Charters, Montmorency, Rivers, Duval, Gurnay, Pinkney, Montford, and Mountney, now to be cited by Englishmen as evidence of coming in with the Conqueror!

Dutch *van*, German *von*, and Italian *di*, *da*, likewise, in the majority of cases, had no more important function than that of the English prepositions, 'of,' 'from,' and 'at'.

Surnames from Buildings. The daily work of many men kept them in close association with some building, and this feature has resulted in the descriptions of diverse edifices being perpetuated in our family names.

Joan ate Barbekane, Kent, 1317. (G.D. 27, m. 20.)
Hen. de la Charyte, Bucks. 1247. (Ass. R. 56, m. 20.) Now Charity.
Rob. de Galilea, Northants. 1294. (G.D. 95, m. 6d.) Now Galilee.
Ric. de Garderoba, Oxf. 1296. (G.D. 96, m. 40.) Now Wardrobe, Wardrop.
Hen. atte Skolehous, Norf. 1349. (G.D. 134, m. 14.) Now Schoolhouse.
Ric. del Smethie, Cumb. 1377. (G.D. 165a, m. 3.) Now Smithee.
Geof. Tolbothe, Norf. 1383. (G.D. 164, m. 43.) Now Tolputt.

No modern survival of Barbican has been noticed. A galilee was a portico or chapel annexed to some cathedrals, and a toll-booth was the office for receiving payment of tolls, and also detaining delinquents. Into this section sometimes fall a few surnames derived from the descriptions of employers, as Vicars, Parsons, meaning the house of the Vicar or Parson.

J. atte Officiales, Lincs. 1349. (Ass. R. 1443, m. 6d.)
Pet. atte Vicars, Yorks. 1379. (Poll Tax, p. 19.)
W. "atte Persones serviens Joh'is Toly de Bolewyk, corveyser," Northants, 1414. (G.D. 195, m. 94.)

Shop and Tavern Signs.[1] In the middle ages when houses were unnumbered it became necessary to distinguish one building from another of similar appearance, by naming them, and as the majority of people could not read, the most convenient form of label for shop and tavern was the pictorial signboard, which became a noticeable feature of the business streets, and so far as inns are concerned, is yet quite common. Like "Fat Jack from the Lord Clive" (see below, p. 168) many a man's secondary designation took the form of a description of the sign under which he worked, and the children taking the father's distinction, the advertisement of an ancient establishment became fixed as a family name. It is hardly to be doubted that numerous animal and other curious names can be explained in this manner.

Gilbert de le Hegle, Suss. 1275. (Hund. R.)
W. del Whythorse, Warw. 1285. (Ass. R. 957. m. 1.)
W. atte Ramme, London, 1320. (Fines.)
Godfrey atte Swan, London, 1337. (Coroner's R.)
J. atte Pye, London, 1339. (Coroner's R.)

It may be noted that Wytehors was a place in Berkshire, 13th cent. (G.D. 36, m. 15).

The hanging signs were often heraldic, the tradesmen adopting as the token of their houses, the ordinaries, charges, and badges, of their overlords, or perchance late masters, and the following list of heraldic emblems is equally a list of known inn-signs, all of which have also been traced as modern surnames.

Animals: Ape, Badger, Bear, Boar, Brock, Buck, Bull, Camel, Catt, Coney, Dear, Doe (Hind, Hart, Roebuck), Dragon, Fox, Griffin, Hedghogg, Lamb, Leopard, Lion, Oliphant (Elephant), Ram,

[1] *E.H.S.*, p. 229.

Squirrel, Stagg, Wolfe. *Birds:* Cock, Crane, Crow, Dove, Eagle, Falcon, Heron, Peacock, Pigeon, Pye, Raven, Rook. *Miscellaneous:* Anchor, Bell, Cross, Devil, Rose.[1]

Some animal names are of the genealogical and occupational or even of the characteristic class, as Hare, *i.e.* 'the heir', and unless the surname can be traced back to the prepositional form it is not possible to say that it is of local origin. Perhaps it is unnecessary to point out that these names, so often erroneously derived from supposed nicknames, should never be assigned to such a source without proof, the probability being so strong that they are of a much more prosaic nature.[2] Surnames might also be derived from names of ships. Hakluyt (*The Principall Navigations*, 1598–1600, II, ii, 156), for instance, relates that at the Azores in 1589, one of the greatest ships was the Falcon of London, she being under a Scottish pilot, who bare her name as his own.

Surnames from Topographical Features. A great wealth of surnames of a most interesting character, both topographically and philologically, are those derived from hill and dale, the forest and the farmyard, such appellatives being most numerous in English, Cornish, and Gaelic, varied by an occasional French or Scandinavian example. The following explanation from the *History of Surnames* (p. 232) may be worth repeating.

"Under the manorial system the territory occupied by a village community was limited by the boundary *marks*, and the arable *land* separated into *fields* to provide for the annual rotation of crops. The open fields were divided into *furlongs* (furrow-long) or *shots* with *head*

[1] *E.H.S.*, p. 231.
[2] *E.H.S.*, pp. 332–7.

lands on which the plough was turned, and the furlongs were split up into *selions*, *lands*, *strips*, *ridges*, or *rigs* of an *acre* or *half-acre* by balks of turf. *Banks* between terraces were called *lynches*, abutting strips were known as *butts*, narrow projecting parts as *spongs*, tongues of land as *steortes*, and odd triangular pieces were described as *gores*. From these italicised terms, common among husbandmen, were derived such surnames, as Acre, Bank, Butt, Field, Furlong, Gore, Halfacre, Head (Headley, etc.), Land, Lynch, Mark, Ridge, Rigg, Shott, Spong, Storte, and Stripp. Sylion as a second name occurs several times in the Salop Subsidy Roll, 1327, but it has not been traced as a modern surname. It is customary to say that such surnames as these were derived from places of residence, but the fact is that the holdings of each labourer being scattered strips, the husbandmen had perforce to live in the villages, and it is much more probable that they were known to their fellow men and the officials of the manor by the descriptions of their land holdings, which in time became their family surnames."[1]

The following short list comprises some less recognisable modern surnames which correspond to the designations of topographical features.[2]

English: Beam (tree); Bottom (a hollow); Flatt (level piece of ground); Gott (drain); Greave (thicket); Hanger (wood on a slope); Heal (corner); Hope (enclosed land); Knagg (pointed rock); Load (leaning wall); Lumb (deep pool); Maw, Mow (stack); Meals, Meols (sandbanks); Parrock (small enclosure); Sales (hall); Sass (sluice); Sheath (spring); Syke (stream); Twitchell (alley); Tye (pasture); Vennel (passage); Wade (ford); Zouch (tree stump).

French: Cowdery (grove of hazel trees); Boyce (wood); Packet (meadow); Tallis (copse); Travers (cross road).

[1] *E.H.S.*, p. 232.
[2] For a longer list, see *E.H.S.*, p. 233.

Cornish: Biscoe (*bos crou*, m. 'dwelling'); Bolland (*polan*, f. 'pool'); Clegg (rock); Gilly (grove); Glyn (woody valley); Loe (pool); Pill (*pil*, m. 'hillock'); Praed (*prâz*, m. 'meadow'); Quick (*gwik*, f. 'village'); Scawen (*scauan*, f. 'alder tree'); Sparnon (*spernan*, m. 'thorn'); Toll (hole); Vease (*vêz*, m. 'open field'); Vose (ditch); Warn (*guernen*, f. 'alder tree'); Woon (*wón*, f. 'a down').

Gaelic: Aird (a height); Barr (hill-top); Benny (*beinnach*, 'hilly place'); Cluny (pasture); Clyne (slope); Cowan (*cobhan*, 'a hollow'); Cran (tree); Currie (*currach*, 'a marsh'); Darroch (*darach*, 'an oak'); Fintray (*fionn traigh* 'white strand'); Glaister (*glas tir*, 'green land'); Inch (*innis*, 'island'); Kelt (*coillte*, 'woods'); Leckie (*leacach*, 'hill-side'); Moy (*magh*, 'plain'); Rait (fort); Reay (*reidh*, 'flat land'); Stooke (*stuc*, 'jutting hill'); Torrance (hillock).

Scandinavian: Beck (brook); Carse (low land along a river); Fell (*fjeld*, 'mountain'); Fleck (*flegg*, 'flat'); Halse (a neck of land); Ing (meadow); Keld (spring); Lund (grove); Scales (*skáli*, 'shepherd's hut'); Slack (shallow valley).

A compound local surname consists of a topographical feature plus a personal name, as Nanjulian (Corn. 'the valley of Julian'); plus a trade, as Trengoff (Corn. 'the dwelling of the smith'); plus an adjective, as Smallpiece, Braithwaite (O.N. *breithr*, 'broad', *thwaite* 'clearing') or Stroyan (Gael. *sruth*, 'a stream', *an*, 'little'); plus a preposition, as Surtees (on the Tees); or plus another topographical feature, as Eskdale (Gael. *uisg*, 'water'), Calder (Gael. *coille*, 'wood', *dar*, 'oak').

There are many English compounds, some of which may be identified at sight, as Bancroft (bank), Culverhouse, Featherstonehaugh, Nethersole, Oxlade, Whinwray; others again have so changed as to present difficulties, such as Pybus (pike-busk) or Metcalf, noticed above (p. 73). One of the commonest of elements was *-house*, which suffering considerable corruption, sometimes nearly faded away, as Dyas (dye-house), Loftus, Salters, etc. See also Rygges (p. 59).

Rob. of ye Duffus (dovehouse), Suff. 1291. (Ass. R. 837, m. 1d.)
Thom. Wodehouse or Wodesse, Norf. 1509. (Pard. R.)

Surnames from Rents. Tenants being so commonly distinguished by descriptions of their lands, it may be surmised that in some cases the most convenient form of identification may have been by specifying the rent, and that in some such manner have arisen surnames, as Fivepeni, Ninepennys, etc.,

Hugh Francservice, Bucks. 1228. (Ass. R. 54, m. 3*d.*)
Thom. Gersoma,[1] Dev. 1327. (E179, 95/7, m. 16*d.*)

If the possibility now expressed is feasible, then the same explanation will serve for such family names, as Sparrowhawk (sometimes reduced to Spark, also a distinct name), Horsenail, Peppercorn, Cummin, Capon, and Barleycorn, all of which were payable for certain tenures, but Sparrowhawk certainly, in most cases, is the O.E. baptismal name, and others are corruptions, Tenpenny being from O'Tiompain (Ir.), and Peppercorn may have been the name of a spicer.[2] Hundredpound, more often written Hunderpound, is suspiciously like Underpound (cf. Underhill), and Thousendpond likewise may be a local description. The fact that Centlivre is to be found, merely points to translation (cf. Twentipens and Vintdeners, p. 86).

Surnames from Trees. Fourteenth-century rolls exhibit numerous descriptions from trees, as atte pertre (pear-tree), atte stok (tree stump), in the wilewes, atte grove, atte park, atter oak, atte apse (O.E. *Æsp*,' the aspen'), atte thorne, etc., and numbers of these descriptions became surnames, as Alder, Ash, Aspen, Beech,

[1] Gersum, a premium or fine paid to the suzerain.
[2] Bardsley (*E.H.S.*, p. 234n).

Birch, Broom, Box, Elm, Hazel, Holly, Maple, Peartree, Plumtree, Shrubb, Sycamore, Tree, Willows and Yew.[1] Possibly O.E. font-names may be the origin occasionally, as Ealdhere, Æsc, Brum, Sigemær, etc. Some aphæretic examples are:—Noakes (atten Oakes), Nelmes (atten Elmes), Nash, Nalder, etc.

W. del Aspes, Cumb. 1292. (Ass. R. 136, m. 41.)
Ph. atte Notebeme (hazel-tree), Glouc. 1327. (Subs. p. 10.).
W. atte Norchard, Glouc. 1327. (Subs. p. 26.)
W. Bitherose, Dev. 1333. (E179, 95/7, m. 22*d*.)

For the description Wood in various languages, see above (p. 86).

Surnames from Rivers and Lakes.[2] Places of occupation and residence were also described by reference to an adjacent river, lake, or ford. Few English examples are noticed, as Derwentwater, Manifold (Staffs.), Tame, Tees, Wye, etc., and perhaps Winsome (Wensum); but in Scotland, where lochs and burns are a charming feature of the country, surnames from such sources are more noticeable, as Blackadder, Calder, Clyde, Cree, Eglin, Frew, Garnock, Gass, Gedd, Liddell, Minnoch, Reyburn, and Rule. Some surnames corresponding to those of rivers may, of course, have other derivations, such as Cam (W. crooked).

(II.*B*) **Surnames from late Place of Residence.** An original description of this class was given to one who having moved from one place to another, became known to the recording clerk or to his new acquaintances as of the country of his birth or of his late town. A good deal of perplexity in identification of these names is due to the fact that numbers of the small villages and ham-

[1] *E.H.S.*, p. 234.
[2] *Ibid.*

lets have disappeared and others of the same name hav
sprung up, thus Oldfield (Holdfield, Aldefield) may b
not only from any one of a number of parishes, but als
from some locality now either non-existent or elusive
Some obviously local surnames have no identifiabl
counterpart on the modern map, such as Rushby,
typical eastern name, Ellershaw, certainly from th
North, or Battiscombe from the south-west. A surnam
like Sutton (south inclosure or town) may be commo
to all the counties of England, but it is distinctly Eng
lish; while others, such as Blomfield may be from eithe
French Blundeville or English Bloomfield, accordin
to its history. Another great difficulty of identificatio
is due to the fact that the original orthographic forms c
the appellative and the locality from which it spran
have developed on divergent lines, thus the Domesda
Book Bodesbi (Lincs.) is responsible for both the moder
place-name Boothby, and the surname Bobby.

Surnames from Countries and Counties.[1] Du
to the large number of aliens permanently settled i
England is a series of surnames, which, in general, ma
be readily identified. The preliminary descriptions, i
Latin, are first noticed in Domesday Book (1086), a
Albertus Lothariensis (of Lorraine); Aluredus de His
pania (of Spain); Rogerus Pictaviensis (of Poictou
Resulting surnames are:—Alman (Germany), Brabe
Champagne (often confused with Champion), Englan
(possibly the meadow-land, see above, p. 26), Hollan
(also perhaps from place-names in Lancashire, Esse
etc.), Ireland, Lorraine, Spain, Scotland (possibly fro
the hamlet in Lincs. or even personal name). In simila
manner surnames corresponding to names of countie
have been obtained.

[1] *E.H.S.*, p. 237.

Arnold de Kent, Notts. 1204. (Cur. Reg. R.)
Walt. de Westm'land killed W. de Rutland, Bucks. 1286. (Ass. R. 65, m. 43.)
Ralph de Wyltschir, Kent, 1302. (G.D. 26, m. 7.)
J. Anglesey, Lond. 1401. (K.B. 9, 191, no. 46.)

Modern directories evidence the following:—Chesher, Cornwall, Derbyshire, Dorset, Essex, Hampshire, Kent, Lancashire, Norfolk, Surrey, Westmorland, Willsher; and from Scotland, Fife. Montgomery is a French local surname which being given to the Welsh county, again became a surname: Ric. Williamson alias Brouderer alias Mongomery, Midx. (K.B. 29, 91, Trin. 26 Hen. 6.)

Surnames have also been derived from divisions and hundreds, as Flegg (hundred, Norf.), Holland (division, Lincs.), Kesteven (division, Lincs.), Lindsey (division, Lincs.), Wayland (hundred, Norf.); and the Scottish examples, Annandale and Tweddle (Tweeddale). The surnames North, South, East and West may be assigned to this section, and sometimes Dyas (Gael. *deas*, 'south').

Surnames from Towns, Villages and Hamlets. In a very large number of cases a person was distinguished by the name of the town or village from which he came, and such address becoming permanently associated with him and his family, now provides a link in a most interesting series of surnames. As explained above one such appellative often sprang from a number of different sources, but others may be identified at sight with one county only, as Bousfield of Westmorland, Wrottesley of Staffordshire, Colgate of Sussex, Godolphin of Cornwall, Brackenbury of Lincolnshire, and Quarmby of Yorkshire.[1]

Many appellatives of this class, although they cannot

[1] A list of 600 such names may be seen in *E.H.S.*, pp. 238–41.

be assigned to any one county, may be tentatively identified with some district, surnames terminating in *-by* (a dwelling-place) are typical of Lincolnshire and the East; those in *-combe* point to the South-West, those in *-thwaite* (clearing), *-twistle* (a fork), *-bottom*, and *-shaw* (small wood) recall the North. The best indication that a surname is of local derivation is obtained from the second element, such as *-bury* (fortified place), *-cott*, *-den*, *-ford*, *-ham* (farm), *-hope* (valley), *-ley*, *-ridge*, *-stead*, *-ton*, *-thorpe*, *-wick* (N. village), and *-worth*, as well as the more distinctive ones already mentioned, and others more obvious. All these simple components undergo considerable variation; *-haugh*, for instance, appearing in such forms as, *-halgh*, *-haulgh*, *-hough*, *-how*, *-ock*, *-ough*, *-ow*, *-up*, in Greenhalgh, Eatock, Hindhough, etc.; or *-ham*, as *-am*, *-hem*, *-man*, *-nam*, *-num*, *-om*, *-um*, in Kingham, Oldman, Hayson, Fortnum, etc.[1]

In Cornwall there are more local surnames proportionately than in any other part of the country, and in general they are most distinctive, although owing to corrupt orthography, the signification is not easily determined with certainty. Prominent first elements are:—*Car-* ('rock' or 'camp'), *Lan-* ('an enclosure' or 'church'), *Pen-* ('head' or 'hill'), *Pol-* (pool), *Ros-* (valley), and *Tre-* (dwelling), as in Carthew, Lambron, Penarth, Bolland, Rosecregg, and Dreadon. Glynne and Pennant may be either Welsh or Cornish, and Pettigrew, a well-known Cornish surname conceivably became attached to the manor in Gerrans, rather than the reverse, and so may not be the Cornish *bedh y grew*, "the crane's grove". The name is now more commonly associated with Scotland, where it is found in records of

[1] Good lists of first and second elements are given in *E.H.S.*, pp. 373–80.

the fifteenth century, but it is not to be inferred that it originated independently over the Border.[1]

Walt. Peticruw, Ess. 1227. (Ass. R. 229, m. 18.)
Walt. Petittru, Ess. 1249. (Cl. R.)
J. Petitru, Ess. 1268. (Ass. R. 237, m. 2.)
Rich. Peticru, Ess. 1283. (Ass. R. 1256, m. 29d.)
Geof. Petitcru, Norf. 1295. (G.D. 47, m. 8.)
Thom. Petycru, —— 1296. (Pat. R.)
Rog. Peticru, Suff. 1298. (Ass. R. 1311, m. 24d.)
Thom. Peticru, St. Monans, 1327. (E179, 87/7, m. 13.)
Thom. Petycru, Somers. 1329–30. (Fine.)
Ran. de Peticru, Helston, Cornw. 1338. (Cl. R.)
Ralph Beddegru, Truro, Cornw. 1338. (Cl. R.)
Sir Thom. Peticru, Kt., Cornw. 1342. (Cl. R.)
Rob. Petycru, Wilts. 1345. (Inq. p.m.)
Rand. Petycru, outlaw, Cornw. 1347. (Blk. Pr. Reg.); 1354 (Pat. R.)
Thom. Peticru, Burngullow, Cornw. 1360. (Blk. Pr. Reg.)
Thom. Pedegru, Ess. 1371. (C.P. 25 (1), 68, 228, 1636.)
J. Peticru, Ess. 1378. (Pat. R.)
Ric. Petegrieu, Lond. 1396. (Cl. R.)

It will be observed that the earliest examples do not come from Cornwall, but from the East, where anything but Cornish origin is to be suspected. The possibility of derivation from the French should not be overlooked. Grue, not only Cornish, is also English and French. Bec-de-Grue (crane's bill), the name of a place (Norm. R. 1195), by assimilation, might easily become *bedh y grew* in Cornwall. The eastern examples may be from petitcru (small growth).

Some of the modern Cornish surnames have taken on

[1] *The Scotsman* (5 Oct. 1931), having refused to accept an origin for Pettigrew outside Scotland, saying that it "seems non-existent in Cornwall", the examples now given will have an added interest. Can these Northern journalists seriously contend that these extracts relate to the progeny of Scotsmen, whose family name is derived from an hypothetical *pett an craoibhe* or Pittencrieff, Dunfermline. Surely, since the earliest Scottish reference is to a priest as late as 1406 (*Papal Petitions*), the probability is that the name came from the south, rather than the reverse, at a time when so few Scots came into England.

such an English appearance as to be very misleading, as Carver (*car veor*, 'the great rock'), Forder (*veor dour*, 'the great water'), Mainprice (*mean prâz*, 'the stony meadow'), Mulberry (*moel vre*, 'the bald hill'), Penmar (*pen maen*, 'the head of the rock'), Treble (*tre bel*, 'the fair town'), and Winter (*gwyn dour*, 'the white water').

From Welsh sources local surnames are comparatively scarce, as Blaen, Bodvill, Breckon, Cardiff, Cardigan, Carew, Cogan, Conway, Dolben, Flint, Gower, Gwinnett, Kennifeck (from Kenfig, Glam., found in Ireland), Kyffin, Laugherne, Llanwarne, Penrhyn, Penrice, Powis, Prendergast, Rawbone (Ruabon), Rumney, Sully, Tanat, Yale.[1]

Scotland provides a considerable number of local surnames identifiable with one county of origin, as Lumsden (Aberdeenshire), Cullen (Banffshire; also possibly Irish), Marwick (Ross-shire), Gilfillan (Wigtownshire), and Wedderburn (Berwickshire). Many Scottish local surnames are of Gaelic origin, as Lendrum (*leathar druim*, 'broad ridge'), but, as may be expected, Norse examples are to be found, *e.g.* Dingwall (*thingvöllr*, 'field of the thing or court of justice').[2]

Local surnames of Irish origin are few, but the following may be examples:—

Adair, Ardagh, Athy, Blaney, Borris, Boyle, Breen, Cashel, Cavan, Costello, Doak (Doagh), Dromgoole, Drummond, Dunhill, Finglas, Galway, Garvey, Kells, Kilcullen, Kilkenny, Limerick, Longford, Lusk, Monaghan, Pallas, Seaton, Weatherston.[3]

Many Englishmen bear surnames derived from place-names in France and Normandy, often now much corrupted.

[1] *E.H.S.*, p. 242.
[2] *E.H.S.*, p. 243.
[3] *Ibid.*

Baskerville (Bacqueville), Brassy (Brecy), Bullen (Boulogne), onyers (Coigneres), Dives, Doyley (d'Ouilly), Molineux (de Molinlles), Money (Monne), Montgomery (de Monte Gomeri), Olley Ouilly), Quarritch (de Quarroges), Quatermass (Quatermare), emper (St. Pierre), Umfreville (Amfreville).[1]

[1] *E.H.S.*, p. 243.

CHAPTER IX

GENEALOGICAL DESCRIPTIONS AND SURNAMES

Group I (Inherited Surnames). Class III. Possibly the most ancient and also the most certain way of identifying a person was to recite his lineage, answering the question—who are his nearest or most important kin? References to the genealogical description in previous sections will have established the pedigree system to be much more prevalent among Celtic than Teutonic or Scandinavian races, so that to-day nearly all surnames of pure Welsh and Irish origin are of this class, and owing to the migration extending over many years, they have spread all over Britain, the Dominions, and the United States of America. In addition, Englishmen largely adopted a modified form of this particular distinction, as did aliens, so that in this division are to be found not only Welsh, Gaelic, and English names, but also French, Hebrew, and appellatives of other races. The result is that genealogical surnames numerically form the second of the four classes in group I (Inherited Surnames) comprising from 30 to 40 per cent of the whole.

Not all genealogical surnames are confined to those derived from the personal names of father, mother, or other relative; occasionally characteristic, local, or occupational descriptions, with the help of the filial desinence, or ancestral prefix, have become genealogical

Surnames of the genealogical class have been subdivided, according to their origin, (*A*) from personal name of male parent, called patronymics; (*B*) from personal name of female parent, called metronymics; (*C*) from personal name of other relative; (*D*) from descriptions or surnames.[1] A few examples of O.E. genealogical descriptions may be seen on p. 25, and of Welsh on p. 50.

(III.*A*) **Surnames from Personal Names of Male Parent.**[2] There are four distinct formations of patronymics.

(i) *Simple formation.* The genealogy having been expressed, at first, in the descriptions, by the employment of a word signifying 'son', as Lat. *filius*, N.F. *fitz*, W. *ab*, Ir. *mac*; or daughter, as Lat. *filia*, W. *verch*, Ir. *ingean*, or descendant, as Ir. *o*, *ua*, etc., a desire for brevity led to dropping the word defining the relationship, resulting in a simple genealogical description or surname indistinguishable from the parental forename, thus 'Willelmus filius Rogeri' became 'William Roger' (1254, Cl. R.)

(ii) *Prefixion.* The filial expression, or part of it, coalesced with the personal name as a prefix, as Fitzgerald, (*a*)Pritchard, (*ma*)Googan (from Mac Eochagáin, (ma)Kewish from Mac Uais, etc. The Latin *filius* became *filz* and *fiz* in O.F., and afterwards *fitz* and *fils*, and joined with the following name, French or English.

J. Fizdieu, Northants., 1303. (Ass. R. 1327, m. 23d.)
J. Fitzherbert or Fiherbert, Derb. 1509. (Pard. R.)

Ireland is the great home of the Fitzes, one person in every 180 being either a Fitzgerald or a Fitzpatrick,

[1] *E.H.S.*, p. 245.
[2] *Ibid.*

actually threatening the supremacy of the O'Briens, O'Neills, and McCarthys. Fitz-names do not point to Norman ancestry, nor to superior family, and there is no reason to suppose that they indicate irregularity in birth. *Fitz* ranks equally with *ap*, *mac*, *son*, etc. in expressing relationship, legitimate and illegitimate.

(iii) *Genitive case ending.* Notwithstanding the disuse of the distinctive words *filius* and *filia* the Latin genitive termination was sometimes retained in the parental name:—

Willelmus Johannis, Glouc. 1159–60. (Pipe R.)
Petrus Bernardi, 1255. (Cl. R.)
Simon Pauly, Warw. 1275. (Hund. R., m. 27.)
Thomas Basily, Cambs. 1345. (G.D. 134, m. 75d.)

The Latin genitive forms have had little influence on surnames, although, since the genitive ending of both the first declension (*e*) and second declension (*i*) was often written *y*, names in modern transcripts may appear as Jacoby, Iweny, etc. (see also below, Mabily, etc.)

In the thirteenth century, the English form of genitive case endings, *es*, *is*, *ys*, and *s* came into official use, but at first more frequently in the names of women, thus 'Robertus filius Radulfi' became 'Robertus Rolle' (Raoul), but 'Matilda filia Radulfi' was written 'Matilda Rolles'. There was no precise rule as to the distinction of genders, many second names of women being without the final sibilant, which, in the thirteenth century, is occasionally to be found added to the surnames of men.

Gervase Ivans, Devon, 1230. (Cl. R.); now Evans.
J. Rolves, Oxf. 1275. (Hund. R.); now Rolfes.
J. Willames, Heref. 1301. (Ass. R. 1322, m. 9.); now Williams.

Possibly in the early instances the terminal *s* was due

to influence of the French nominative singular ending, seen in names like Jacques, Gilles, Jules, etc. The names of men with the affixed sibilant became more plentiful in proportion in the following century. By the sixteenth century the final *s* was occasionally written *ce* and *se*.

J. Adamsse, Glouc. 1471. (K.B. 29, 113, 11 Edw. 4.)
W. Pearce, or Perce, or Peirs, or Perse, or Peirce, or Peirse, or Pearse, adm. B.A. 1601. (Reg. Univ. Oxf., ii, pt. iii, 221.)

The terminal *s* is not always the genitive ending, but may be due to metathesis, as Cripps from Crisp, an apocope of Crispin: *e.g.* Rob. Cryps or Crysp, Oxf. 1293 (G.D. 92, m. 12d.).

Modern orthography sometimes doubles the *s*, as Jefferiss. The sibilant following the *k*-sound has given names terminating in *x*, as Simcox, Madox, etc. That names terminating in *s* are not more prevalent is due to the fact that the genitive case ending was by no means in general use in colloquial speech, for instance, in *Robert of Gloucester* (13th c.) the uninflected 'possessive' occurs 'for marie love', 'the quene fader', etc.

Regarding the possibility of final *s* being an ellipsis for *son* it seems impossible to make any definite statement, but the following examples may be considered.

Thomas Wyllyams alias dictus Thomas Wyllyamson, Midx. 1503. (K.B. 29, 139, Hil. 18 Hen. 7.)
Rob. Nycoll, Nicols, or Nicolson, Ess. 1509. (Pard. R.)

Wyllyams may here be an example of apocopation, but equally well an independent formation, indicating by genitive inflection "son of William". So also in the case of Nicols, but there can be little doubt of the apocopation in "Mary Evans alias Evanson", 1598 (C54, 1588).

In fourteenth-century records a limited use of the O.E. terminal letter *n* of the oblique cases is to be noticed, thus the Gloucester Subsidy Roll for 1327 has Marioten for Mariotas, Amycen for Amyces, Hugin and Huwen for Hughes, Rosen for Roses, Geffen for Geffes, Watten for Wattes, and Maggen for Magges. That the termination is not the diminutive suffix is clear from such entries as Alice la Reven (*i.e.* the Reves; p. 21c.).

(iv) *The filial desinence.*[1] A second compound method of forming genealogical surnames was by the use of the filial desinence, as O.E. *sunu*, 'son' or 'descendant'; O.N. *sonr*; early examples of which have been given on pp. 25, 31.

From the early twelfth century until the fourteenth the filial suffix rarely appears in the records, and then mainly in the North.

Rog. Dodesune, Shrops, 1283. (Cl. R.)
Gamel Lokeson, Cumb. 1292. (Ass. R. 136, m. 5.)
Sim. Maistergefreison, Northants. 1321. (Ass. R. 1381, m. 39.)
W. Ithelsone, Chesh. 1334. (Chester 29, 45, m. 14.)

The last example is a hybrid, Welsh and English, like Evanson. Sometimes terminal *son* signified 'daughter'. "Margaret Richardson and Elizabeth Richardson" were daughters of Richard Johnson alias Jackeson (Chesh. 1568; Anc. D., A 12206.) 'Daughter' was also used to form patronymical descriptions in like manner to 'son'.

Edith Leofrices docter Locces.[2] (Thorpe, p. 636.)
Leflet Ecregeles docter, Hants. 1066. (Wint. Dom.)
Marg. Simdoghter, Durh. 1378. (Surt. Soc. lxxxii, p. 144.)
Joan Jakdoghter, Lincs. 1384. (Ass. R. 1496, m. 1.)

[1] *E.H.S.*, pp. 172, 248.
[2] The form employed also in descriptions of servants, see below, p. 160.

In view of our great alien population, it may be of interest to notice that the French had no filial desinence, but the Germans used *-sohn* in addition to other equivalents, *e.g.* the genitive in *-s*, as Sieviers; the *-ing*, *-ung*, suffixes, as Karling, Eysink, Adelung, etc., and the -er suffix, as Wilhelmer.[1] There is some reason to believe that many of our names in *-son* are of Danish or Dutch origin.

(III.*B*) **Surnames from Personal Names of Female Parent.**[2] There are but three distinct formations of this subclass, prefixion of a word expressing the relationship not having been noticed.

(i) *Simple formation.*

Willelmus Alis, —— 1068. (Fr. Docts., Round.)
Gilbertus Milisent, Warw. 1288. (Ass. R. 1279, m. 3d.)
David Susan, Cornw. 1327. (Subs. 87/7, m. 13d.)

Examples of fusion with Dame, in general, products of Gloucestershire, are Damedith, Damemme, Damarie, Damelin, etc. (Subs. 1327.) Alis may not be here the feminine name, it being in early days, like Emma, Ethel, and Maud, epicene, that is common to both sexes.

(ii) *Genitive case ending.* (See also above, p. 134.)

Rog. Susanne, Warw. 1275. (Hund. R. m. 21.)
Reg. Mablii, Cambs. 1275. (Hund. R.)
Hug. Mabely, Bucks. 1286. (Ass. R. 65, m. 29d.)
Rog. Sibile, Lincs. 1327. (E179, 135/11, m. 9.)
Laur. Sybely, Norf. 1345. (G.D. 134, m. 62d.)

Mabil, in the genitive, is inflected both according to the first declension as Mabille or Mabilie, and the second, as Mablii; and was often written Mabely, a

[1] Solmsen, p. 183.
[2] *E.H.S.*, p. 249.

modern surname being Mabley. Cf. Jacoby (see page 134).

The terminal *s* is scarce in early metronymics, corresponding to the O.E. practice of rarely inflecting feminine substantives in the genitive case. Emms and Orables are to be found in the Hundred Rolls (1275), but the first was often a male name, and possibly the second also. Janes is not uncommon, but evidently as a variant of Jones. An undoubted example of a metronymic is Katheryns, which occurs in the Rutland Subsidy Roll, 1523 (165/112).

(iii) *The filial desinence.* The filial suffix in conjunction with the mother's name is not uncommon, as Beatson, Tillotson (from Matilda), etc.

J. Letticesone, Beds. 1316. (G.D. 1, m. 20.)
Hen. Dameanneissone, Derb. 1330. (G.D. 123, m. 18d.)
Ric. Littelemmessone, Northants. 1335. (Ass. R. 1400, m. 92d.)
J. Mariesone, Beds. 1341. (G.D. 1, m. 64d.)
J. Maggotessone, Cambs. 1347. (G.D. 134, m. 36d.)

Thomas Letesone Barret,[1] Northumb. 1339. (G.D. 132, m. 14.)

Agn. Letesdoughter, Norf. 1343. (G.D. 49, m. 58.)
Isab. Gracedoughter, Beds. 1347. (G.D. 134, m. 51d.)

Metronymics are no indication of irregular birth, as erroneously supposed by some writers. The name of the most important parent formed the genealogical description or surname, *e.g.* John Biset was son of John de Wotton and Ela Biset, his *wife*, Worc., 1300 (Inq. p.m.). Among Welshmen and Jews it was common practice for a son to take the name of his mother (*e.g.* Liquorish, see p. 48).

(III.*C*) **Surnames from Personal Names of other Relatives.**[2] Names only of suffixal type can be

[1] The form employed also in descriptions of servants. (See below, p. 160).
[2] *E.H.S.*, p. 250.

determined by inspection, and they are found to be much more prevalent in the North than in the South.

W. Boiestepsone, Bucks. 1247. (Ass. R. 56, m. 45.)
Adam Musefader, Cumb. 1279. (Ass. R. 131, m. 11d.)
Hugh Gilbertmagh (*i.e.* brother-in-law), Cumb. 1292. (Ass. R. 136, m. 8.)
Thom. Saundrebrother, Cumb. 1346. (G.D. 165a, m. 25.)
Adam Martynbarn, Yorks. 1359. (G.D. 141a, m. 36.)

In the same way, stepdaughter, wife, child, cousin, and neve, may be found compounded. A longer form corresponding to that employed in descriptions for servants (see below, p. 160) has been noticed above for daughter (p. 136) and son (p. 138) and occurs in the case of a wife: Johanna Joneswif Willeson (*i.e.* Joan wife of John Wilson), Yorks. 1358 (G.D. 145, m. 14d). A few surnames of this type have survived, as Hitchmough, Watmough, and variants.

(III.*D*) **Genealogical Surnames from Descriptions or Surnames.**[1] There are three distinct formations of this subclass, simple formations falling into other sections.

(i) *Prefixion.* (1) Prefix + characteristic description.

M'Edesey (*mac an Deisigh*, 'son of the Decian'); also Deasey.
Mac Gill (*mac an Ghaill*, 'son of the foreigner'); also Gill.

(2) Prefix + occupational description.

M'Evelly (*mac an mhilidh*, 'son of the knight'.)
Mac Scollog (*mac an scoloige*, 'son of the farmer.')

(ii) *Genitive case ending.* This section is difficult to illustrate satisfactorily owing to the impossibility of distinguishing between (*a*) plural *s*; (*b*) excrescent *s*;

[1] *E.H.S.*, p. 250.

and (*c*) genitive case ending. (1) Characteristic names from relationship (subclass *G*, p. 111), as Neaves, Eames, Couzens, Brothers, seem to exhibit an excrescent *s*, but Crookshanks is a plural form.

(2) Local. A final *s* is not uncommon in surnames derived from topographical features, but again it is impossible to point to an instance which exemplifies genealogy beyond doubt. Analysis has shown that the probability of names from topographical features having been originally plural forms is not more than 3 in 100.

J. Kers, Oxf. 1275 (Hund. R.): cf. W. de le Ker, Cambs. 1275 (*ibid.*)

Such names, rare in the thirteenth-century lists, have become very prevalent, as Banks, Brookes, Cairns, Clowes, Hargreaves, Holmes, Ings, Knolles, Lillies, Lowndes, Nares (W. Knari, Warw. 1275, Hund. R., m. 42d.; O.E. *knar*, 'rugged rock', 'tree stump'); Oakes, Raikes (*rake*, 'a rough path'); Rhodes or Royds ('clearing'; now also the name of a parish in Lancs.), Sykes, and Yates. "The terminal *s* can hardly be the genitive formation in these instances, and since, in considerable measure, the plural formation has been ruled out, probably, in a number of cases, the *s* is a meaningless excrescence, the addition of a terminal sibilant being not uncommon with uncultured people."[1] It is possible also that occasionally *s* is all that is left of 'house'. (See Rygges from Rygehouse, pp. 59, 123).

(3) Occupational. Descriptions derived from trades, offices, etc., are also found with final *s*.

Sibil Barbours, Dev. 1327. (E179, 95/6, m. 25.)
Ric. le Clerikes, Glouc. 1327. (Subs. p. 16.)

[1] *E.H.S.*, p. 251.

While such names cannot be in the plural number, additional difficulties of classification arise owing to confusion with the feminine agential suffix, and to the fact that occupational descriptions are often indistinguishable from personal names. In a list of Huntingdonshire sokemen appear Thom' le King, Elena fil' Rad' le King, Hugo King, Bele Kinges, and Felicia Kinges (Hund. R., p. 609). Here Kinges seems to be an occupational description with genitive case ending, but it may be nothing more than the baptismal name Kin(g). Other personal names, Lord, Quen, and Cniht, have their occupational doubles, as Lord, Queen, and Knight, and in the *Hundred Rolls* (1275) may be seen Loverdes (Lords), Quenes, and Knictes, the function of the *s*, whether genitive case ending, or an excrescency, being uncertain. Alice le Driveres and Julian' le Smithes possibly exhibit the feminine agential suffix, which is sometimes written *-es* as in lyonnes, duches, etc.

Modern surnames of this class are Husbands, Masters, Mellers, Parsons, Reeves, and possibly Vickress and Yeamans: but such names may be from local descriptions; cf. atte Persones (see above, p. 119). A case of the preservation of the O.E. terminal *n* in the Glouc. Subsidy Roll, 1327 has been noticed above (p. 136).

(iii) *Suffixion of relationship.*[1] (1) The filial desinence is rarely found in records of later date than the Norman conquest until the fourteenth century, when it began to appear freely in the northern lists. Son (and more rarely daughter) may be affixed to a description or surname consisting of:

(*a*) A characteristic adjective:—

Alex. Scotson, Yorks, 1379. (Poll Tax, p. 206.)

[1] *E.H.S.*, p. 252.

(*b*) A locality:—

(α) From country, as Ric. Waleson, Lincs. 1380–1. (Cor. R. 82, m. 11d.)

(β) From place. Consecutive entries are Thomas de Mosergh and Hugh Moserghson, Cumb. 1333. (E179, 90/2, m. 21d.)

Agn. Horsecroftesdout', Beds. 1316. (G.D. 1, m. 16.)
Cecilia Fisshemarketdoughter, Yorks. 1366. (G.D. 145, m. 52d.)

(*c*) An occupation:—

Osb. Smythessone, Lincs. 1255. (Cl. R.)
Adam le Smythessone, Cumb. 1292. (Ass. R. 136, m. 6.)
Geof. le Deyesone, Berks. 1295. (G.D. 96, m. 13.)
J. Shepbirdsone, Cumb. 1339. (G.D. 132, m. 7.)

Modern surnames of this class are, Clarkson, Herdson, Hindson, Smithson, Taylorson, and Wrightson.

Surnames compounding filial desinence and genealogical description or surname, as Williamson are indistinguishable from (*A* iv) or (*B* iii), above pp. 136, 138.

(2) Relationship other than filial may be compounded in like manner with descriptions or surnames derived from:

(a) A characteristic adjective:—

Johannes Barnefadir, Yorks. 1379. (Poll Tax, vi, 147.)

(b) A locality:—

Alicia Graynewyfe (cf. W. de Grayne), Yorks. 1379. (Poll Tax, vi, 30, 147.)

(c) An occupation:—

Robertus Parsonbrother, Yorks. 1379. (Poll Tax, v, 11.)
Agnes Milnerwyf, Yorks. 1379. (*Ibid.* vi. 326.)
Johannes Vikercosyn, Yorks. 1379. (*Ibid*, vi. 333.)

Compound descriptions with similar second elements, the first elements being genealogical surnames, are indistinguishable from subclass (*C*) above, p. 138.

The principal influences in the formation of genealogical surnames have been the prevalence of Anglo-Saxon, Norse, Norman, Cornish, Welsh, Scottish, Irish, and Hebrew names, as the following examples illustrate.[1]

Anglo-Saxon (O.E.) Influence. (i) *Uncompounded Surnames.* Many of the O.E. monothematic names of one thousand years ago, such as the following examples, can be found preserved with little or no change in our surnames.

Barne, Bass, Bate, Bole, Brand, Burro, Cabe, Cane, Clare, Deor, Dunn, Else, Fin, Fisc, Frome, Golde, Grima, Har, Hyne, Lang, Man, Orde, Pipe, Pymma, Smala, Sport, Thynne, Tunne, Wade, Walle, Wod.

(ii) *Compounded Surnames.* The following modern surnames are typical of those derived from O.E. dithematic baptismal names:—Aldridge (*eald*, *ric*); Brightman (*beorht*, *man*); Colvin (*cól*, *wine*); Dumphrey (*dóm*, *frith*); Elphick (*ælf*, *wig*); Freeburn (*freo*, *brand*); Gotobed (*gode*, *beorht*); Hurlin (*herle*, *wine*); Jarrold (*gær*, *weald*); Kimball (*cwen*, *beald*); Leverick (*leof*, *ric*); Orgar (*ord*, *gær*); Redmond (*ræd*, *mund*); Theobald (*theod*, *beald*); Whatman (*hwæt*, *man*). Surnames in *-ing*; Billing, Dowding, Golding, Living, Tilling, Waring, Wilding. The probability of other origins is particularly strong in the case of *-ing*-names. Some local surnames are compounds of a monothematic personal name and the suffix, as Spalding, Kipling, Pickering, Gidding, etc., other compounds have not been identified, as Gowering and Pudding.

[1] Fuller lists, *E.H.S.*, pp. 252–7.

Ailword Pudding, 11th c. (Thorpe, pp. 634, 636.)
Hugh Pudding, Yorks. 1230. (Pipe R.)
J. Puddyngg', Bucks. 1320. (Ass. R. 71, m. 3.)
J. Pudding, Heref. 1412. (G.D. 189, m. 27.)

Norse Influence.[1] "These surnames are usually indistinguishable from those of Anglo-Saxon derivation, but the following are probably of Norse origin; Ankettle, Arkcoll, Arkell, Askill, Aslac, Gemmell, Grimkil, Inger, Kettle, Magniss, Oskell, Osmund, Patrick, Rankil, Usborn, although not all are to be found in modern lists."

Norman Influence.[2] "The following examples are representative of the surnames derived from the Norman-French appellatives which became established in spite of the overwhelming popularity of William, John, Roger, Robert, etc.: Ansell, Arment, Bertin, Bisset, Blaze, Blease, Bowkett, Buckett, Challand (Jolland), Chamen, Elwes (Heloise), Girardot, Guerin, Guichard, Guille, Lancelin, Mayo, Minett, Pepin, Perowne (Perrin), Poyntz, Wydowe (Guy)."

Cornish Influence.[3] "Few distinctive Cornish personal names have survived as surnames, and these are mainly appellatives formerly borne by saints: Arthur, Gluyas, Jennifer (Guinevere), Jewell (Brit. Judicael or Juhel), Keverne, Key, Tangye (*i.e.* Tanguy, common in Brittany), Ustick (probably adjectival from Just)."

Welsh Influence.[4] The majority of Welsh surnames are of the genealogical class, but they are by no means restricted to those of native origin; English, Norman, and Hebrew names being largely adopted, resulting in the production of hybrids, such as Badams (W. and

[1 2 3] *E.H.S.*, p. 254.
[4] *E.H.S.*, p. 255.

Heb.), Bedward (W. and E.), Probert (W. and Norm.-Teut.). Notwithstanding the patriotism of the Briton, great numbers derived their names from the Normans, as is evidenced by the modern army of Williams and Richards. Some examples of surnames derived from Welsh personal names follow:—

Anyon (Einion), Beevor (ab Ivor), Bethell (ab Ithel), Blood (ab Lloyd), Bowen, Bunner, (ab Inyr), Bunyan (ab Einion), Flewellin (Llewelyn), Griffin or Griffith, Heaven (Evan), Onion (*eynon*, 'just'), Palin (ap Heilin), Parry (ap Harry), Pendry (ap Hendry), Powel (ap Howel), Press (ap Rees), Proger (ap Roger), Pugh (ap Hugh), Pumphrey (ap Humphrey), Rees, Rhys or Rice, Thelen (Llewelyn).

Some Welsh names, like the ubiquitous Evan and Owen, may be found in nearly every English county and have spread all over the world.

Hen. Bunion, Beds. 1204. (Cur. Reg. R.)
Amicia Yevan de Galys, Suff. 1371. (G.D. 152, m. 43.)
Dav. app Price, Kent. 1498. (K.B. 9, 415, no. 41.)

Scottish Influence.[1] Modern Scottish surnames of this class are mainly derived from Gaelic (originally Irish), Norse, Anglo-Saxon, and in comparatively recent years, again Irish personal names. Some distinctive Scottish surnames are:—

Aitchison, Beattie, Dickie, Dougall, Farquharson, Finlay, Grierson, Jamieson, Kirsty (Christopher), Macalister (Alasdair), MacAlpine, MacAusland, Macfarlane (Parlan), McInnes (Aonghas), McKenna (Ionaigh), MacTavish (Thomas), Paterson, Shaw (sometimes local).

Irish Influence.[2] "Irish surnames of true native origin are nearly all of the genealogical class, formerly distinguished by the use of Mac and O, now often in

[1] [2] *E.H.S.*, p. 256.

part elided or dropped altogether, the corruptions being even more remarkable than anything found in English nomenclature." Under English influence and legislation numbers of Irishmen took English names, but others anglicised the native names, which was done in various ways, as O'Donoghue from Ó Donnchadha, Cowie from Ó Cobhthaigh, Barnacle, a supposed equivalent of Ó Cadhain, Wyndham from Ó Gaoithin, Carlton from Ó Caireallâin, Newcombe from Ó Niadhôg. Curiously, O'Brisset is not Irish but a corruption of the Huguenot name Aubrisset.[1]

Hebrew Influence.[2] A number of surnames originate in biblical personal names as Absalom, Jeremy, Joachim, Moyse (Moses), Salmon (Solomon), etc., but they do not necessarily point to Semitic ancestry. Hebrew names may be hybridised by the use of the English filial desinence, as Abrahamson and Jobson; or a N.F. diminutive, as Jobling and Tobin; or a Welsh prefix, as Abadam. Some surnames of Jewish origin are not Hebrew, as Liquorice from Licoricia (Gr.), and others again of Semitic appearance may be of a quite different nature.

J. de Abrahame de Abrahame (now Abram), Lancs. 1436. (K.B. 9, 231, no. 112.)

[1] P. A. S. Phillips, *John Obrisset*, 1931.
[2] *E.H.S.*, p. 256.

CHAPTER X

OCCUPATIONAL DESCRIPTIONS AND SURNAMES

Group I (Inherited Surnames). Class IV. In group 1 the fourth method of identifying a person was a reply to the question—what is his vocation? The descriptive answers, often applicable to son as well as to father, had a tendency to become accepted as the family designation, and finally the heritable surname. This class has been estimated to include from 12 to 20 per cent of the total family appellatives,[1] which are found to be mainly English, although a few Latin, French, Cornish, Welsh, and Gaelic examples can be traced. The names of this class include many archaic words and form an interesting study, the principal formations being the single-element noun, as Grieve (bailiff); noun + noun, as Church-ward; noun + suffix, as Limn-er (illuminator of MSS.); or verb + suffix, as Web-ster (weaver).

In addition to official, professional, and military appointments, and the numerous manual callings, a number of surnames seem to be derived from mock or imitation offices; consequently the following subclasses have been adopted: (*A*) from office or profession; (*B*) from mock office; (*C*) from military rank; (*D*) from trade or vocation.

(IV.*A*) **Surnames from Office or Profession.** In

[1] *E.H.S.*, p. 257.

this subclass may be found surnames perpetuating the vocations of ecclesiastical, legal, and manorial officials, such as Bailey, Chamberlain, Chaplin, Cleaver (macebearer), Corner (coroner), Deemer (judge), Hamper (Hanaper), Munk, Pope, Potticary, Priest, Proctor (an attorney in a spiritual court), Scholar, Sellars (the cellarer), Sermoner, Sewer, Spicknell (spigurnel, a sealer of writs), Vavasseur, and Waight (watchman).

Wulfric Judex (the Judge), Norf. 1205. (Cur. Reg. R.)
Adam le Maunsiple (college servant), Bucks. 1340. (Ass. R. 74, m. 12d.)

Scottish examples are: Bailie (also local), and Dempster. Irish: Cleary (clerk), Davin (*daimh*, 'poet'), and Ward (*bhard*, 'bard'); and a Hebrew surname of the class is Cohen (priest).[1]

(IV.*B*) **Surnames from Mock Office.** A number of surnames, such as King, Prince, Duke, Earl, and so on, manifestly have not been derived from persons holding such titles, and it is necessary to search for other origins. So important a part did mysteries, miracle plays, and pageants take in the lives of our forefathers that it is not improbable that some of the leading characters such as king, queen, devil, angel, and dragon, became associated with the particular actors who sustained such rôles year after year, and established as surnames. Further there were various festivals like the May crownings, when king and queen, although elected for the year, may have retained their nominal distinctions. King, although an early personal name (see Ching, p. 31 above) is so common that perhaps its origin can best be explained by occupation of some mock office. The name survived in Latin, as Rex (sometimes Rekes,

[1] *E.H.S.*, p. 258.

hopelessly confused with Raikes; see p. 140), and possibly in French, as Roy, which in Ireland is used for both M'Elroy and Royston. Prince occurring as early as 1166 is a puzzle. It cannot be the O.E. name Prin +s, because the final sibilant did not appear until a century later, and it may be a pageant name, or in some cases a tavern name, or the bearer may even have been servant to a prince (A groom was called Whiteknight!). Dukes, barons, and lords, were leaders, often in a very small way, and are found with the article *le*, as are Earl and Bishop, but Queen, Marquis, Earl, Lord, Knight, Bishop, and Abbot, all approach the form of O.E. personal names as they appear in Domesday Book and other early records.

Reg. le Duc, Cambs. 1199. (Cur. Reg. R.)
Alan King, Lincs. 1205. (Cur. Reg. R.)
Matilda le Quen, Oxf. 1275. (Hund. R.)
Rog. le Erle, Cambs. 1275. (Hund. R.)
Walt. le Dragon, Lincs. 1275. (Hund. R.)
W. Dragoun, Bucks. 1294. (G.D. 96, m. 9.)

Mary Woodfield alias Queen of Hell, Surr. 1788. (Croydon Par. Reg.)

(IV.*C*) Surnames from Military Rank.[1]

Johannes le Squier, —— 1208. (Rot de Obl.)
Ricardus le Archer, Worc. 1238. (Cl. R.)
Robertus le Mangoneys, Glouc. 1290. (G.D. 89, m. 4.)

Possibly the last description is not derived from mangonel, the engine of war designed to sling stones, but from Lat. *mango*, 'a trader'.

Some modern surnames of this subclass are: Alabaster, Banister (the arbalester or cross-bowman), Bower (in some cases), Bowman, Camp (soldier),

[1] *E.H.S.*, p. 259.

Chevalier, Footman, Halfknight, Kemp (soldier), Knight, Pickman (pike), Scorer (spy), Slinger, Squire, Thane (thegn). A Cornish example is Marrack (soldier); an Irish representative is Colgan (*colg*, 'swordsman'); and possibly a Norse name is Skiddie (*skyti*, 'shooter').

(IV.*D*) **Surnames from Trade or Vocation.**[1] The manual labourers provide the majority of occupational surnames, the largest proportion being derivatives of the noun or verb + suffix type, the remainder being compounds (noun + noun), with a few exceptions, as Day (dey, 'a dairywoman'), Faraday (chapman), Husband, Ladd (serving man), Smith, Ward (guardian). *Cornish:* Annear (*an eure*, 'the goldsmith'), Angove (the smith), Tyacke (*tyac*, 'farmer'). *Irish:* Gow (*gobha*, 'smith'). *Welsh:* Crowder (*crythwr*, 'a fiddler'). *Scottish:* Caird (tinker).

In this class may also be included surnames derived from certain degrees of feudal tenants, since by their tenures they obtained their livelihood, as Cotter, Drengher, Franklin, Prudhomme (Fr. 'freeholder'), etc.

Names from Employers. One of the most interesting series of occupational surnames includes those derived by adding the vocation to (i) the personal or hypocoristic name of employer, as Isakman, Mathewman, Blissewenche; (ii) the surname of employer, as J. Whytacresman, Warw. 1375 (Ass. R. 1481, m. 6d). See also Multonman, Dryffeldman, p. 115; (iii) the occupational description of employer, as Priestman, Vicariespenser, and Ladyman.

Owing to genitival inflection being rare, Joneman, for instance, being as correct as Jonesman, such appellatives are often indistinguishable from (*a*) characteristic names, *e.g.* Smallman, the man of Small (pers. name), is also the

[1] *E.H.S.*, p. 259.

small-holder; (*b*) local names, as perhaps Pyntelboy (the wood of Pintel?; cf. Littleboy from Littlewood, and Coppedeboie, 'coppice wood'); (*c*) genealogical names, *e.g.* Blacman, the man of Blac, is also the O.E. personal name Blacman; (*d*) occupational names, thus Garlikman, the man of Garlec, is also the garlick-vendor. Of surnames being compounds of work and man, a further selection will be found on pp. 154-5.

Since surnames as well as personal names of employers are permissible in composition of this nature, curious problems in meaning arise, for instance, while W. Yongegrom may have been William the young groom, and less likely the groom of William Yonge, he was much more probably William the groom of Yonge, or but for scribal carelessness, William Yonge, groom.

It will be realised that very great difficulty exists in the determination of the exact nature of compounds with vocation as second element, and the following list will provide food for conjecture.

Ric. Steresman, Yorks. 1168. (Pipe R.)
Ric. Coppedeboie, Oxf. 1175–6. (Pipe R.)
W. Echemannesmai, Dev. 1175–6. (Pipe R.) M.E. *may*, 'man'.
W. Cristeman, Hants. 1202. (Cur. Reg. R.)
Rob. Caldeswain, Bucks. 1247. (Ass. R. 56, m. 11d.)
W. Paksweyn, Bucks. 1247. (Ass. R. 56, m. 11.)
Emma Broneman, Bucks. 1261. (Ass. R. 58, m. 25d.) Genealogical, cf. Rog. fil' Brunmanni, Hants. 1174–5. (Pipe R.)
Rog. Bukkeman, Cumb. 1278. (Ass. R. 133, m. 16d.)
Walt. Sleghgrom, Bucks. 1286. (Ass. R. 65, m. 40d.)
J. Wysman, Berks. 1292. (G.D. 91, m. 1.)
J. Colswayn, Wilts. 1292. (G.D. 91, m. 4d.)
Walt. Brounstracour, Surr. 1292. (G.D. 36, m. 51.)
W. Nicholfforester, Cumb. 1292. (Ass. R. 136, m. 5.)
Thom. Vycaryesmon, Warw. 1295. (G.D. 96, m. 24.)
W. Fadirman, Lincs. 1299. (G.D. 97, m. 8d.)
Rob. Hendeman, Hunts. c. 1317. (G.D. 1, m. 6.)

W. Williamsquier, Kent. 1317. (Ass. R. 1366, m. 66.)
J. Johanesprest, Bucks. 1332. (Ass. R. 73, m. 3d.)
Ad. Shortman, Ess. 1330. (G.D. 123, m. 7.)
Ric. Lucyeheghes, Dev. 1333. (Subs. 95/7, m. 10.)
W. Wounderman, Wilts. 1335. (G.D. 120, m. 8d.)
Sim. Isakman, Warw. 1336. (Ass. R. 1400, m. 127d.)
J. Williamscartere, Bucks. 1341. (Ass. R. 73, m. 17.)
Warner Slyladde, Hunts. 1343. (E179, 122/4, m. 4.)
J. Thyngman, Suff. 1349. (G.D. 134, m. 70.)
J. Quickman, Cambs. 1346. (G.D. 134, m. 32.)
Ralph le Vicariespenser, Norf. 1349. (G.D. 134, m. 17.)
Adam Hardymarchant, Yorks. 1363. (K.B. 29, 20, m. 20d.)
J. Asscheman, Ess. 1381. (E179, 107/68.)
J. Megreman, Northants. 1390. (Ass. R. 1501, m. 10.)

Agential Suffixes.[1] The principal suffixes found in surnames indicating occupation are: English: *-er*, *-ier*; fem. *-ess*; mf. *-ster*; with variants. Cornish: *-ar*, *-er*, and *-or*. Welsh: *-or*, *-ur*; and *-er* often occurs under English influence. French: *-and*, *-ier*; fem. *-esse*.

A selection of modern surnames follows:—

-and, -ant. Marchand, Servant.

-ar, -ard. Erroneous spellings for *-er*.

-er. Biller (billman?), Bowdler (buddler, 'a worker in iron ore'), Cadger (hawker), Catcher (huntsman), Cramer and Creamer (a pedlar), Dawber (plasterer), Dubber (O.F. *doubeur*, 'a repairer'), Ewer (a servant who supplies washing utensils), Fanner (one who winnows grain with a fan), Firminger (O.F. *fromageur*, 'a cheese-maker'), Fower (cleaner), Graver (turf-digger), Hiller (slater), Jester (a reciter of romances, or buffoon), Keller (bargeman), Kidder (huckster), Knowler (bellman), Leaper and Leper (dancer), Messer (mower), Offer (Fr. *orfevre*, 'a goldsmith'), Pargeter (plasterer), Pester (Fr. 'a cook'), Poyser (weigher), Raper (roper), Sloper (clothier), Squiller (scullery servant), Stringer (one who makes strings for bows), Tenter (cloth-worker), Vacher (cowherd), Waferer (cake-maker).

These names have to be distinguished from local

[1] *E.H.S.*, p. 286.

descriptions in *-er*, as Docker (Westm.) and Dummer (Hunts.). Occasionally *-er* is a variant of *-hewer* or *-herd*, q.v. An early form was without the final *r*, representatives being Flawn, Hawke, Hogsflesh, Poulter, Webb, etc.

Rob. le Gigelere, Cambs. 1275. (Hund. R.)
W. Gygel, Cambs. 1346. (G.D. 134, m. 33.)
Thom. Parment or Parmenter, Northants. 1509. (Pard. R.)

Sometimes under Cornish influence final *e* was written *a*, as Walt. le Webba, Cornw. 1332 (G.D. 120, m. 23.).

-iar, -ier, -iour, -yar, -year, -yer. Collier and Cullyer (maker of wood charcoal), Hilliar, Hillyar (tiler), Lockyear, Paviour.

Rob. le Helyere, Wilts. 1332. (G.D. 120, m. 4d.) Cf. Corn. Helyar.
Isab. Herberiour, Derb. 1368. (Ass. R. 1472, m. 31.)

-or, -our, -ur. Harpur, Mellor (one who collects honey).

Eylmer le Tywlur, Bucks. 1247. (Ass. R. 56, m. 45d.)
Pet. le Playtour, Beds. 1319 (G.D. 1, m. 26.)

-ster, -ister, -istor. Feminine agential suffix attached to verbs, as Baxter, Blackistor (bleacher), Brewster, Fewster (maker of saddle trees), Shapster (dress-maker), Thackster (thatcher).

The feminine suffix ultimately came to be used indiscriminately with *-er*, as an agential ending irrespective of gender.

Geva la Upholdestere, Beds. 1297. (G.D. 96, m. 41d.)
Walt. le Blobystere, Warw. 1297. (G.D. 96, m. 39d.)
Cf. W. le Blubure, Oxf. 1275. (Hund. R.)

In documents of the thirteenth and fourteenth centuries use of the French *-eresse* is to be noticed.

Mariota le Tayleresse, Warw. 1275. (Hund. R., m. 9.)
Juliana le Regrateresse, Oxf. 1293. (G.D. 92, m. 8d.)

Surnames of Celtic origin are:—*Cornish:* Bather (coiner or banker), Cauntor (singer), Hellyar (hunter), Sayer (artisan). *Welsh:* Thirteenth-century examples are: Heusawr (the herdsman), Seythor (*saethwr*, ('archer'), Spedor (*spadwr*, 'gelder'). *Irish:* Gleasure (glazier), Gosnell (*góiséir*, 'hosier'). Faber (smith) is a rare Latin example.

Compound Occupational Surnames. Second elements are: *-herd*, *-hewer*, *-knave*, *-lad*, *-maker*, *-man*, *-mason*, *-master*, *-monger*, *-seller*, *-smith*, *-ward*, *-wife*, *-woman*, *-wright*, and variants.

-ard, -art, -er, -erd, -ert, -ett. See *-herd.*

-ger. See *-hewer.*

-herd, -ard, -art, -er, -erd, -ert, -ett, -hard, -head, -itt (the keeper or tender of a flock): as in Calvert, Coulthard, Coward, Fowlherd, Geldart, Gelderd, Gozzard (goose-herd), Hoggett, Hoggitt, Lambert, Oxnard, Stoddart, Swinnart, Weatherhead.

-hewer, -er, -ger, -ier, -year, -yer (one who cuts or shapes): Wooder, Woodger, Woodhewer, Woodyer, etc.

-knave (servant or menial; obs.). Durknave. Lad was also used, but does not seem to have survived.

Gilb. le Horseknave, Cumb. 1292. (Ass. R. 136, m. 41.)

Alan Horsenknave, Cumb. 1292. (*Ibid.*)

J. Hunte alias Slaughtyrladde, Soms. 1346. (K.B. 9, 229, no. 187.)

-maker. Slaymaker (a slay is a weaving instrument).

Ibota Arkmaker, Yorks. 1379. (Poll Tax, v, 26.)

W. Materasmakere, Warw. 1383. (Ass. R. 977, m. 20.)

The second word is sometimes dropped, as J. Materas, Beds, 1400. (G.D. 190, m. 3.)

-man (vassal or servant): Ackerman, Charman, Cogman (cog, a kind of ship), Cowman, Flatman (several definitions), Gooseman, Henchman (groom), Inman, Ironman, Knapman (hammerman), Pepperman, Runciman, Shearman, Silkman, Templeman, Wainman (wagoner), Wayman (hunter), Yeatman (gatekeeper). It will be seen that these names may be derived from the material worked, as Flaxman; the actual work as Wakeman (watchman); and the place of work, as Hallman.

Exceptions: (i) *-man* is sometimes the O.E. element, as Seaman for Seman, a personal name. (ii) A corruption of *-man* is *-ham*, as in Kitchingham, 'the kitchen man'; alternatively *-man* may be a corruption of *-ham*, as in the local surname Deadman for Debenham. (iii) *-man*, like *-er*, *-maker*, and *-monger* may be elided, but identification is difficult.

Rob. le Slaughtere, Suff. 1336. (G.D. 64, m. 11.)

(iv) *-man*, like *-page*, *-swain*, and other vocations, is often affixed to the personal name of master, as exemplified above, p. 151.

-mason. Woodmason.

-master. Rob. Ploghmaystre, Yorks. 1297. (Subs. W. Brown.)

-monger (dealer, trader). Fishmonger, Fleshmonger (Hund. R.), Isemonger (iron).

Walt. le Flexmongere, Beds. 1318. (G.D. 1, m. 24.) Flax or flesh?

Matil. Heringmongere, Glouc. 1327. (Subs. p. 7.)

-monger like *-maker* is sometimes elided. Confusion occurs (*e.g.* Garlek), with not only genealogical surnames, but also characteristic appellatives (from crying wares, see p. 110), and occupational names (from shop signs); but the distinction is very slight.

Joan Stockfish, Dors. 1371. (Fines, ii, 123; E.A. Fry.)

Thom. Smere, Norf. 1473. (K.B. 29, 113, Mich. 13 Edw. 4.)

Pet. Powerfysshe, Lond. 1500. (K.B. 29, 139, 16 Hen. 7.)

-seller. Thom. Barkseller, Suff. 1372. (S.C.2, 203/60, m. 2d.)

-smith. Arrowsmith, Greensmith, Nasmith (knife-smith; Bardsley).

-vassal. Thom. Durevassal, Warw. 1305. (Ass. R. 965, m. 1.); cf. Durknave.

-ward (guardian or watchman). Hayward (a manorial officer), Millward, Woodward. (Note: *-ward* is confusable with *-weard*, as in Dorward.)

-wife, as in Huswyff, a description common to both sexes.

Phil. Huswyff, tailor, Lond. 1446. (K.B. 9, 256, no. 87.)

cf. J. Clerk alias dictus Northerione, huswyffe, 1467. (K.B. 29, 139, East. 7 Edw. 4.)

-woman. Joan Chapwyman, Kent. 1315. (G.D. 26, m. 14.)

Laur. Stelewymman, Ess. 1346. (C.P.40, 342, m. 178.)

W. Stelewoman alias Steleman, Ess. 1582. (Fines, p. 262.)

-wright (artificer). Arkwright. Cheesewright, Plowright, Slaywright, Tellwright (tilemaker), Wainwright (wagon-builder).

-year. See *-hewer*.

Exemplification of Middle English. It is said that

many hundreds of readers searched literature to obtain chronological examples illustrating the use of words for inclusion in the monumental N.E.D.; but no one made any examination of the vast store of ancient court manuscripts deposited in the Public Record Office, beyond such as have been transcribed and printed, consequently a great wealth of valuable material remains unused. Words like Blubure (1275), and Blobystere (1297) are not to be found in the Dictionary, and numerous others have not been traced. Some are, of course, really French, as Oysilour, 'a fowler', Myre, 'a physician', and perhaps Baysere and Gorier.

W. le Allere, Warw. 1336. (Ass. R. 1400, m. 125.)
Hen. le Baysere, Herts. 1333. (G.D. 22, m. 13d.
Sam. le Briggewrithe, Bucks. 1247. (Ass. R. 56, m. 44d.)
Rob. le Buckede, Notts. 1301. (K.B. 27, 163, m. 30d.)
J. le Bukkemongere, Warw. 1302. (Anc. D., A6378.)
Hen. le Butor, Dev. 1204. (Cur. Reg. R.)
Alice le Cabeler, Bucks. 1294. (G.D. 95, m. 7d.)
Sim. le Cuperer, Bucks. 1247. (Ass. R. 56, m. 47d.)
Mich. le Draguner, Lincs. 1302. (Ass. R. 1327, m. 7d.)
J. le Duddere, Warw. 1311. (K.B. 27, 204, m. 19.) A cloth-worker.
Hub. le Duggere, Oxf. 1310. (K.B. 27, 201, m. 63d.)
Rob. le Floppere, Ess. 1287. (K.B. 27, 103, m. 9.)
Alice le Gorier, Beds, 1317. (G.D. 1, m. 21.)
Arnulph le Gowyer, Northants. 1272. (Ass. R. 1221, m. 4.)
Isab. le Harpestre, Dors. 1292. (K.B. 27, 131, m. 21d.)
Thom. le Miriourmaker, Warw. 1273. (K.B. 27, 5, m. 25.)
Rob. le Moldewerper, Yorks. 1298. (K.B. 27, 154, m. 22d.) Mouldwarp, 1325.
Thom. le Myre, Bucks. 1296. (G.D. 96, m. 31.)
Warin le Nattere, Lincs. 1302. (K.B. 27, 170, m. 49.) Netter?
Nich. le Oyelymakere, Worc. 1293. (G.D. 92, m. 3.)
Thom. le Oylemaker, Beds. 1336. (G.D. 1, m. 59.)
Eudo le Saumplariar, Oxf. 1294. (K.B. 27, 142, m. 6.)
Alex. le Sheresmyth, Cumb. 1292. (Ass. R. 136, m. 23d.)
W. le Sleywryghte, Bucks. 1271. (Ass. R. 60, m. 28.)

Rog. le Waddestere, Lincs. 1306. (K.B. 27, 185, m. 51.)
Thom. le Zuller, Glouc. 1324. (Ass. R. 1381, m. 63.)

Any opinion on isolated examples can be little more than conjecture, *e.g.* an alleyer was a merchant, but allers were 'clogs' in the North. Bayser means 'kisser', absurd as a description, unless it was a supposed synonym for the English Kisser, *i.e.* the maker of cuishes (thigh armour). Buckmonger was probably a dealer in lye for bleaching, and Cabeler may be nothing more than 'cobler', whilst Cuperer, looking like 'the cupper' or 'bloodletter', so necessary in the days of gargantuan feasting, may be merely 'the cooper'. For Gorier and Gowyer, may be compared O.F. *goherier*, 'harness maker', and Zuller introduces dialect, a zull being a plough in the West Country.

Further secondary descriptions of persons provide a large number of words of earlier date than traced by the dictionarian, a selection of which follows.

Agn. la Bokbyndere, Oxf. 1295. (G.D. 96, m. 20d.)
Ralph Bokelerpleyer, Warw. 1382. (Ass. R. 974, m. 3.) A fencer.
Ph. le Charetter, Cambs. 1306. (K.B. 27, 185, m. 39.)
Ric. le Cheyermakyere, Oxf. 1293. (G.D. 92, m. 2d.)
Rob. le Clymbere, Cumb. 1292. (Ass. R. 136, m. 57.)
Rob. le Climber, Bucks. 1314. (Ass. R. 70, m. 2.)
In the Hakonar Saga (13th c.) is named one Hallvarthr Bratti (the climber).
Ric. le Clotmonger, Oxf. 1293. (G.D. 92, m. 12d.)
Thom. le Coylter or Quelter, Berks. 1291. (G.D. 89, mm. 10, 13.) A quilter.
Rog. le Feddere, Glouc. 1291. (G.D. 89, m. 3d.)
Nich. le Freyterer, Warw. 1309. (K.B. 27, 196, m. 39d.) *i.e.* fraterer, one in charge of refectory.
H. le Gerthmaker, Beds. 1321. (G.D. 1, m. 30d.)
Rob. le Helyere, Wilts. 1332. (G.D. 120, m. 4d.) A thatcher.
Gilb. le homburghmaker, Warw. 1304. (K.B. 27, 176, m. 5.) A collar maker.

Ric. le Hundreder, Warw. 1262. (Ass. R. 954, m. 11d.) A bailiff.

J. le Mustarder, Beds. 1317. (G.D. 1, m. 24d.)

W. le Ostricer, Soms. 1204. (Cur. Reg. R.) A keeper of goshawks.

J. le Palefreyur, Warw. 1278. (Ass. R. 1228, m. 58.)

J. le Pastemaker, Hunts. 1349. (G.D. 134, m. 48.)

Dav. le Pessoner, Berks. 1291. (G.D. 89, m. 13.) A fisher.

Agn. le Shypestere, Dev. 1335. (G.D. 120, m. 21d.) A dressmaker.

Ralph le Smokere, Bucks. 1271. (Ass. R. 60, m. 15.) Curer or smock-maker?

Pet. le Spitelman, Norf. 1203. (Cur. Reg. R.)

Hen. le Swerdslypere, Cumb. 1292. (Ass. R. 136, m. 14d.) A sword-sharpener.

Geof. le Swymmere, Hunts. 1289. (K.B. 27, 118, m. 31d.)

W. le Syhgter, Beds. 1308. (G.D. 1, m. 4d.)

J. le Taborer, Beds. 1327. (G.D. 1, m. 33.) A drummer.

J. Tothedraghiere, Cambs. 1371. (G.D. 152, m. 18d.)

W. le Trowyere, Worc. 1296. (G.D. 96, m. 33.) A thrower (pottery-worker).

Sim. le Weler, Bucks. 1340. (Ass. R. 74, m. 10d.) A wheelwright.

J. le Wol Sweyngere, Dev. 1327. (G.D. 120, m. 21.) A flax-cleaner.

Asselota la Wymplestere, Cumb. 1292. (Ass. R. 136, m. 23.)

Rog. le Yacker, Leic. 1306. (Ass. R. 467, m. 17.)

CHAPTER XI

ACQUIRED SURNAMES

Group II, Class I. Self-Assumed Surnames. With the exception of recent enactments controlling aliens there have never been any statutes which regulate the gift, assumption, or change of either personal or family names in England or Wales; and ecclesiastical canons only partially control the conferring of first names, not dealing with surnames at all. Any right one may have to personal or family name must therefore be based either on common law precedents, if such written decisions exist, or on the customs of the people.[1] By a most sensible pronouncement of a jury empanelled in the year 1267 it can be gathered that in London, at any rate, it had become acknowledged that a man's true second-name was that of his father, but, as late as the sixteenth century, Coke, L. C. J. held a surname to be of little consequence compared with the christian name, "as a man cannot have two names of baptism as he may have divers surnames". The modern legal view is that "a man may assume any name he pleases in addition to or substitution for his original name; and in adopting even the name or combination of names by which another person is already known he does not commit a legal wrong against that person".[2]

[1] For a full account of the legal status of surnames, see *E.H.S.*, pp. 381–428.
[2] Sir H. H. Shepherd, LL.D., 1912.

Except in a few special circumstances, there being no restriction on the assumption or change of surnames, it is not surprising that a good many people followed their own inclinations. In the system of classification presented above (p. 98), such self-assumed names have been divided into eight sub-classes:—(*A*) Ecclesiastics; (*B*) Theatrical Artistes; (*C*) Authors; (*D*) Business men; (*E*) Private Persons; (*F*) Slaves; (*G*) Refugees; (*H*) Aliens.

Anciently, change of second name was common among ecclesiastics,[1] and in later years, as is known to every one, theatrical artistes, authors, and business men, in many cases, have likewise disguised the identity of their families, and in some instances the new names have ultimately been adopted as surnames, as Wyndham, Irving, etc.[2]

With reference to class (*F*) slaves, upon manumission, frequently took the names of their masters, and the practice also prevailed in our courts of distinguishing a servant by the name of his employer.[3] In a simple type of description the servant was called by a compound in which his vocation was attached to the employer's personal name, with or without the genitive inflection, a curious feature derived from a longer one, thus W. Stevenknave Paynson, that is William the knave of Steven Paynson appears elsewhere on the roll as W. Stevenknave (Yorks. 1352; G.D. 145, m. 21.) giving a clear indication as to the nature of a very much misunderstood class of name. For instance, Bardsley gives Blisswench as a nickname signifying 'the blithe wench', but actually Bliss was a feminine personal name.

[1] *E.H.S.*, p. 264.
[2] *E.H.S.*, p. 265.
[3] *E.H.S.*, pp. 266, 348.

J. Pren, blissa vx' eius, Worc. 1295. (G.D.96, m. 14.)

Alice Blissewenche (1275) was, therefore, Alice the wench of Bliss. In like manner Adam Millenpage, Cumb. 1336 (G.D. 128, m. 1.), was Adam the page of Miles. This aspect of name formation has been amply exemplified above (p. 151), but a selection of illustrative entries may be included.

"Thomas of the parsones de Lutlyngton", Beds. 1330. (G.D. 124. m. 3.)

"Will'us Bacoun de Swynesheued et Thom' Williamesman Bacoun", Cambs. 1343. (G.D. 134, m. 45.)

"BlakeAleyn de Jernemuth et BlakeAleynesman". Bucks. 1349. (G.D. 134, m. 59.)

"Walt' Jonsabynesman & Will' ffullere Jons'uant Sabyne", Oxf. 1375. (K.B. 29, 28, fines.)

"Will'ms voc' syre Joh'n yoman the Roos", *i.e.* William the yeoman of Sir John Roos, Lincs. 1402. (E370, 3/4, m. 2d.)

"Ric'us Kent Joneseruant Ewode de Hardegrave in com' Suff' ploughman", *i.e.* Richard Kent, servant of John Ewode of Hargrave, 1408. (G.D. 200, m. 6.)

"Joh'es Cowper capellanus, Joh'es Vycarman serviens eiusdem Joh'is Cowper, laborer, Elena Vykermeyde serviens eiusdem Joh'is Cowper, spynster." Derb. 1442. (K.B. 29, 91, Trin. 20 Hen. 6.)

Classes (*G*) and (*H*) call for no special remark, the change of name by refugees and aliens coming under the notice of every one. By the Aliens' Restriction Act, 1919, unauthorised assumption of surnames is prohibited.

Class II. Reputed Surnames.[1] Surnames falling into this division are of two classes; (*A*) Of persons who have no surnames at birth, as bastards; and (*B*) Of persons whose surname is unknown, as foundlings. Such names form a very considerable proportion of the

[1] *E.H.S.*, p. 266.

total, and have greatly influenced the nature of our surnames, being the cause of much misunderstanding.

The numbers of children born out of lawful wedlock in the past formed a considerable proportion of the population, the statistics fifty years ago recording about 6 per cent in England, 10 per cent in Scotland, and 2 per cent in Ireland, "the actual ratio of persons of illegitimate birth in Scotland being very much smaller owing to the laws of the country wisely legitimating base-born children by the subsequent marriage of the parents". Formerly it was quite usual for the bastard to take the name of his father, but the modern practice is for the "love-begot" to acquire by repute the patronymic of the mother.

With regard to foundlings, it is only the extraordinary mortality, reaching 99 per cent in Dublin in the eighteenth century, that has saved the nomenclaturist from absolute bewilderment. As the matter stands, the possibility of name-creation in favour of a deserted child must not be overlooked. The authorities sometimes displayed originality in their choice, manufacturing a new appellative of undisguised nature as Lost, Found or Nameless, but more often some existing name or word was adopted. Of known surnames, many of those of past or present notabilities were given a new lease of life, as Pembroke, Vernon, Wickliffe, Nelson, Chaucer, Cromwell, Kneller, and so on. Other foundlings received as labels dictionary words, beasts and birds being popular, and no doubt many supposed ancient nicknames, as Leopard, Snake, Goldfinch, or Sturgeon, are of comparatively recent origin, due to the fertile brain of a parish officer.[1]

[1] For an account of foundlings' names, *E.H.S.*, pp. 268–270.

CHAPTER XII

CURIOUS DESCRIPTIONS AND MISUNDERSTOOD NAMES

Deceptive Surnames. To the superficial modern reader many of the old names are most misleading, for instance, John le Boxere of Essex, 1329 (G.D. 123, m. 7) and Adam le Bruser of Bucks, 1261 (Ass. R. 58, m. 24) at once bring to mind visions of hard-bitten, bare-mitted pugilists; but long before the noble art had been introduced, 'to box' meant to bleed by cupping, this being an interesting early example of the word, and the *bruser* was possibly the burser or treasurer, metathesis of letter *r* and a vowel being common, but it is unsafe to jump to conclusions.[1]

If names were what they appear to be to the modern eye, we should have to classify with Don Juan and Blue-beard, John Sevenloves of Suffolk (1467; G.D. 207, m. 7), but his surname is perhaps merely another of the many corruptions with the common O.E. deuterotheme, *-leof*, or it may be nothing more than a mis-spelling of Sevenhowes. Corrupt orthography is most deceiving, thus to one who has read in "Cocke Lorelle's Bote" of Gogle-eyed Tomson, might suppose that Sweiveleyes also described a gentleman's optics, but actually it is an early form of Silsoe (Beds.), and so it is not to be con-

[1] Cf. Julian le Brozer, Wilts. 1278 (S.C2.209/51.)

cluded that Robert Boystart'[1] had become notorious by stealing a 'wain's piece', or that 'Thomas sans bracys' lived in danger of revealing secrets to the world, he was quite (h)armless as a careless speaker might say.

Rob. Boystart', Bucks. 1271. (Ass. R. 60, m. 22.)
Thom. sans bracys, Hen. III. (Ass. R. 61, m. 6d.)

Stop-gaps. The public archives, printed and manuscript, are replete with curious secondary descriptions, some being due to misunderstanding arising from the clerk hearing for the first time a surname derived from some strange baptismal or place-name, others again being stop-gaps filled in by the scribe to give his document a semblance of completeness, in cases where a name was non-existent or not forthcoming. Distinctions of this nature can sometimes be detected by their appropriateness.

Alan Cuttepurs, hanged by the Prior of Coventry for stealing bread, 1262. (Ass. R. 954, m. 56d.)

Geoff. Helpmself, a thief, Cumb. 1278. (Ass. R. 133, m. 28.) He occurs again under the same name in the King's Bench, 1289. (K.B. 27, 121, m. 40d.)

Thom. Purskeruer, *i.e.* Cutpurse, arraigned for horse stealing, Yorks. 1357. (G.D. 141a, m. 21.)

J. Brekepark, broke a park at Worth, Suss. 1373. (Pat. R.)

Hen. Chopchirch, chopchirch, with other chopchurches, was accused of trafficking in ecclesiastical benefices, Beds. (G.D. 209, m. 48.)

At a gaol delivery at Bedford, 3 Aug. 1323, a number of millers being arraigned for burglary and cattle stealing, four named John apparently had no surnames, for they were entered as J. molendinarius, J. fil' H. molend', J. Berlicake, and J. Flour (G.D.1, m. 45d). It is not

[1] *c* is often indistinguishable from *t*; and 'tart' is actually 'carter'.

wise, however, to be too certain that a description is a nickname, thus Nicholas Blackleech, who was doctor of physic to Henry VIII, derived his appropriate but misleading surname from the Blacklache (black lake).[1]

Scribal Humour. The want of surnames in the thirteenth and fourteenth centuries is evidenced by some, if not all of the following descriptions, which have a temporary appearance, although others may be corruptions of local or genealogical surnames, *e.g.* Bredwater was a variant of Broadwater in Sussex (1441; K.B. 9, 239), and in similar manner, it may be surmised, that 'Bread and Ale' arose.

Geoff. le Petit kookeliko, Bucks. 1241. (Ass. R. 55, m. 26d.)
Walt. Gobythesti, Bucks. 1261. (Ass. R. 58, m. 21.)
Walt. Gobythestyk, Warw. 1262. (Ass. R. 954, m. 64.)
J. Hoppeinthedust, Warw. 1262. (Ass. R. 954, m. 60d.)
Alice Rydebythekyng. Northants, 1278. (C.P.40, 26, m. 13d.)
Hen. Drink al up, Ess. 1281–2. (Fines.)
Alan Outwitheswerd, Westm. 1290. (G.D. 69, m. 2.)
Hen. Dedeinthenest, Westm. 1290. (G.D. 69, m. 3.)
W. Gobytheway, Shrops. 1293. (G.D. 90, m. 1.)
Rob. Lokeinthewynde, Northants. 1324. (Pat. R.)
J. Twowynterold, Ess. 1327. (E179, 107/13.)
W. Bringhamtogedere, Warw., 1329. (K.B. 27, 275, m. 34.)
Rog. Withesorehand, Notts. 1330. (K.B. 27, 282, m. 125.)
Rog. Byndedeuel, Norf. 1332. (K.B. 27, 289, fines.)
Ralph Lightintheheued, Cumb. 1334. (C.P. 40, 333, m. 405.)
Rob. Boltupright, Glouc. 1335. (K.B. 27, 222, m. 96d.)
Adam Yat godmade, souter, Yorks. 1379. (Poll Tax, v, 425.)
Thom. Bydeawhile, Heref. 1519. (K.B. 9, 476, no. 98.)
J. Abovethemoone, a London murderer, Notts. 1601. (K.B. 9, 715, no. 213.)

It is unlikely that any one of these make-shifts ever attained to surnominal distinction, although Twoyearold runs through several centuries, and Boltupright

[1] See Bardsley, under Blackledge.

occurs several generations later in Warwickshire. Strange as such epithets appear at sight, some are perhaps no more than corrupt place-names, others again, are twists invented by a humorous registrar to amuse his fellows. That the scribes did not hesitate to enliven the dry-as-dust proceedings by witty interpolations, we have occasional unmistakeable reminders, for instance the Curia Regis Roll for 1201 dubs Hugh de Castelliun, *mirabilis potator*, 'a marvellous great drinker,' and the same record for 1205 has "Hubertum de Sancto Quintino et Sire Agnetem viraginem suam" (his shrew), and again in 1206, facetiously refers to a Norfolk attorney, as the Earl of Salisbury, and to yet another (Bucks.) as Suspirium et Fletus, 'a sighing and weeping,' perhaps a play upon his name, and in one place he is called Dolor. A clerk called Bon Christian is also designated by antiphrasis Mal Christien, and Nequam Christianus.

Fictitious names were permitted for sureties; everyone has heard of John Doe and Richard Roe, and equally popular with early attorneys were Bat, Cat, Fox, Box, and other convenient monosyllables. In entering up such figments the rhyming principle was frequently adopted by the poetical scribe of the thirteenth-century Assize Rolls, and in one case six consecutive lines terminate with Rob. Knape and Nic. Ape; J. Stok and Ralph Brok; W. Pye and Adam Flye.

It cannot be doubted that some of the entries on the rolls are solely due to the inventive genius of the scrivener, others being epithets considered appropriate by acquaintances, usually called nicknames, and in the following section will be found examples of both descriptions.

Nicknames. A nickname, formerly an eke-name, *i.e.* added name, according to modern understanding is a term which may be defined as "a dispensable appellative of an individual used as an alternative to his personal name or surname or both".[1] Such epithets occasionally appear in the public records, and may be anything but complimentary.

Joh'es Roys Godgarlek, Kent. 1304. (G.D. 26, m. 10.)

J. Blackteghlere valentum de Arundel, Kent. 1305. (G.D. 26, m. 39.)

Agn. de Elmestowe dicta Drinkhalday, Hunts. 1308. (G.D. 110, m. 1.)

Joh'es Gola d'cus Fendecause, Dev. 1327. (G.D. 120, mm. 16d, 19.)

J. Shirreve d'cus le Northerne, Wilts. 1335. (G.D. 120, m. 8.)

Walt. Spore d'cus Joliwatte, Suff. 1346. (G.D. 134, m. 26d.)

W. Bernard alias dictus Blanklok, alien, 1348. (Cl. R.)

Hen. Bonde fil' Nich'i Bonde d'cus Trilontheberye, Thom. de Lodelowe d'cus Whirlinthecole,[2] Norf. 1351. (G.D. 134, m. 18d.)

Ric. Fletcher, monoculus, Hants. 1402. (E370, 3/4, m. 1.)

J. Arderne alias dictus Longe John of Ireland, 1422. (K.B. 9, 220, no. 12.)

J. Smyth al' d'cus Braynles, Suff. 1423. (G.D. 201, m. 5.)

Ric. Hobbes al' d'cus Blakehikkes (*i.e.* Black Richard), Bucks. 1438. (K.B. 9, 230, no. 157.)

Sir Humfrey Stafford "commonly called Humfrey Stafford with the silver hand," Staffs. 1473. (K.B. 9, 337, no. 6.) Many centuries before, there had been an Irish king, Nuadhat, who was nicknamed Airgellamh, because he had an artificial silver hand: Cóir Anmann, 12th cent.

Katerina Sengilwoman alias d'ca Keterina the flying gost, Surr. 1492. (K.B. 29, 121, m. 27d.; and 139, East. 7 Hen. 7.)

Margaret Rowlynson alias d'ca Spotted Jane, Chesh. 1606. (Chester 21/2, p. 33b.)

Pet. Darke alias le dumbe man, Dev. 1670. (Assizes, 23/1.)

Most of the above-named persons were offenders, and

[1] For a full discussion on the meaning of the word, see *E.H.S.*, pp. 326–8.

[2] The earliest example of the phrase 'tril' or 'tirl on the berry' in the *N.E.D.* is dated 1519. It occurs several times in 16th cent. plays, and is thought to correspond to 'troll the bowl', *i.e.*, 'pass round the wine'. 'Whirl in the cole' presumably indicates a driver of a whirlcole, a kind of conveyance.

while the invention of aliases by an active criminal himself can be accepted, the alternative epithet might be due to the playfulness of the recording clerk, certainly we may rest assured that a certain gentleman accused of horse stealing did not himself assume the last distinction in the following string.

J. Cook alias Dale alias Thirnyng alias London de London, cook alias Theef, 1476. (G.D. 210, m. 1d.) Cf. Helpmself, above, p. 164.

Even as late as the eighteenth century a man's surname might be completely submerged under a flood of more descriptive nicknames, for instance, the incumbent at Esher, in 1772, had to register the burial of "Bacchus alias Hogtub alias Fat Jack alias John from Ld. Clive at Claremont". True nicknames such as these rarely became surnames.

Analysis of Names. Before any serious attempt can be made to determine the nature of a curious compound name it should be divided into its elements. This is a procedure which suffers from uncertainty, the obvious being very often incorrect, thus the description Cartrope, rather than Cart-rope is more likely to be Car-trope, *i.e.* Carthorpe. Having tentatively divided the name, the next step is to compare it with others having the same components, when some indication may be obtained of its origin. For instance, the names with second-element *-god* have much more the appearance of corrupt personal names than those with *-horn*, which savour rather of a local source, yet sometimes *-god* may be merely *-cot*, and the compound a place-name. The *Hog-* and *Kill-* names are also mainly local, but occupational descriptions are also indicated, as with Hogsflesh and Killbullock. The following lists are included to provide the student with a little preliminary food for conjecture, in digesting which it is hoped he will derive both pleasure and an insight into the composition of surnames.

-amour. Ric. Finamur, Dev. 1204. (Cur. Reg. R.)
Gilb. de Fenamore, Wilts. 1275. (Hund. R.)
And. Pleynamur, Suff. 1275. (Hund. R.)
J. Paramour, Lincs. 1275. (Hund. R.)
Note: Finmere is a place in Oxfordshire; Pleynamur, see p. 86.

-buck. Alice Turnebuk, Yorks. 1206. (Cur. Reg. R.)
J. Sherebuck, Northants. 1294. (G.D. 95, m. 6.)
Steph. Lakebuk, Wilts. 1299. (G.D. 98, m. 4d.)
J. Terbuk or Tarbox, Hunts. 1487. (K.B. 29, 117, m. 17.)
Note: Tarbock is a Lancashire parish.

Cat- Ralph Cattessone, Wilts. 1103. (Lib. Winton.)
Agnes Kattesnese, Lincs. 1275. (Hund. R.)
Rob. Cateson, Lincs. 1327. (Subs. 135/11, m. 5d.)
Pet. Catesbrother, Norf. 1342. (G.D. 49, m. 55.)
Thom. Cattestree, Shrops. 1448. (K.B. 29, 91, Hil. 26 Hen. 6.)
Ric. Catskin, Yorks. 1575. (Grimsby Par. Reg.)
Note: *Cat-* is an extremely common element in place-names, cf. Catesby.

-cat. Ric. Pilecat, Norf. 1166. (Pipe R.)
W. Wyldecat, Bucks. 1228. (Ass. R. 54, m. 4d.)
Rob. Pusekat, Northumb. 1256. (Ass. R.)
Geof. Kepecat, Norf. 1275. (Hund. R.)
J. Pulcat, Suff. 1337. (C.P. 40, 306, m. 117.)
Thom. Pilkat, Yorks. 1360. (G.D. 145, m. 20d.)

-corn. W. Spelkorn, Flanders, 1163. (Hoorebeke, p. 64.)
W. Barlicorn, Lincs. 1233. (Cl. R.)
W. Haccorne, Wilts. 1278. (S.C.2. 209/51.)
J. Malicorn, Glouc. 1327. (Subs. R., p. 13.)
Nigel Holdecorn, Lincs. 1333. (Subs.)
W. Pellycorn, Beds. 1336. (G.D. 1, m. 59d.)

Rob. Oldcorn, Norf. 1345. (G.D. 134, m. 63.)
Adam de Skillingcorne, Lancs. c. 1350.
Agnes ine Skylycorn, I.O.M., 16th c. (*E.H.S.*, p. 185.)
cf. Gilb. Skeylehorn, Derb. 1508. (K.B. 29, 140, m. 32); Rob. Pellycan, Cambs. 1346. (G.D. 134, m. 34).

Crack- J. Crakesheld, Norf. 1355. (G.D. 139, m. 22.)
Hen. Crakestryng, Yorks. 1364. (G.D. 145, m. 44.)
Sim. Crakplace, Cumb. 1428. (G.D. 11, m. 8.)

Dog- Rob. Doggefel, Somers. 1201. (Cur. Reg.)
Adam Doggetayl, Warw. 1286. (Ass. R. 1272, m. 16.)
Rog. Doggemouth, Warw. 1287. (K.B. 27, 106, m. 27.)
J. Doggeleg, Suss. 1296. (Subs.)
Alice Dogerel, Beds. 1321. (G.D. 1, m. 32d.)
Hugh Doggetail, Worc. 1327. (Subs.)
Hen. Doggesone, Lancs. 1332. (Subs.: Rylands.)
Ric. Doggeskyn, Yorks. 1346. (Pat. R.)
W. Doggepintel, Leic. 1361. (Ass. R. 466, m. 21.)
Ric. Dogman, Yorks. 1379. (Poll Tax, p. 79.)

Drink- Walt. Drinkemilk, Warw. 1262. (Ass. R. 954, m. 50d.)
W. Drynkepeny, Norf. 1274. (K.B. 27, 7, m. 12.)
J. Drinkwater, Shrops. 1275. (Hund. R.)
Elewan Drynkhale, Norf. 1275. (Hund. R.)
Geof. Dringedregges, Lincs. 1280. (K.B. 27, 52, m. 3.)
Hen. Drink al up, Ess. 1281–2. (Fines.)
W. Drynkwel, Beds. 1371. (G.D. 152, m. 31d.)
Adam Drynkfast, Yorks. 1358. (Ass. R. 1131, m. 6.)

-fish. J. Spetefysh, Worc. 1295. (G.D. 96, m. 22d.)
Hen. le Elfissh, Kent. 1311. (G.D. 27, m. 3.)
Pet. Powerfysshe, Lond. 1500. (K.B. 29, 139, 16 Hen. 7.)

-foot. Leggefot, Dev. 11th. c. (Thorpe, p. 645.)
Willemot Quikeuot, Dev. 11th. c. (Thorpe, p. 646.)
Ailric Bulefot, Dev. 1175. (Pipe R.)
Nich. Batfot, Suff. 1201. (Cur. Reg. R.)
Rob. Gildenefot, Norf. 1201. (Cur. Reg. R.)
Hen. Pancefot, Dors. 1204. (Cur. Reg. R.)

W. Halfot, Surr. 1205. (Cur. Reg. R.)
Odo Alefot or de Aleford, Northants. 1205. (Cur. Reg. R.)
W. Leyfot, Bucks. 1247. (Ass. R. 56, m. 39.)
Rog. Joyfot, Bucks. 1247. (Ass. R. 56, m. 39.)
Hugh Proudfot, Bucks. 1261. (Ass. R. 58, m. 28d.)
Phil. Swyftfoth, Suff. 1272. (Ass. R. 1221, m. 2.)
Ralph. Goldefot, Bucks. 1286. (Ass. R. 65, m. 22.)
Walt. Lyghtfot, Bucks. 1293. (G.D. 92, m. 1.)
W. Hoggesfot, Berks. 1294. (G.D. 96, m. 6d.)
J. Harefot, Northants. 1297. (G.D. 96, m. 48d.)
Alan Wagfot, Cumb. 1303. (G.D. 10a, m. 3.)
Note: In many of these cases *-fot* is *-ford*, and the name of local origin, *e.g.* Batfot or Bateford, now Battisford. In other instances, as the first example, *-fot* indicates a survival of an O.E. name.

-god.

Phil. fil' Holigot, Staffs. 1200. (Cur. Reg. R.)
Rob. fil' Swinegot, —— 1204. (Cur. Reg. R.)
Ric. Livegod, Warw. 1204. (Cur. Reg. R.)
W. Norgod, Suff. 1204. (Cur. Reg. R.)
Hen. Fyndegod, Ess. 1272. (Ass. R. 3, m. 13.)
Rog. Getegod, Cumb. 1278. (Ass. R. 133, m. 21.)
Ric. Maydegod, Bucks. 1286. (Ass. R. 65, m. 36.)
J. Muchegod, Worc. 1295. (G.D. 96, m. 15.)
J. Wynegod, Hants. 1337. (G.D. 120, m. 10.)
Thom. Oldegod, Suff. 1349. (G.D. 134, m. 26.)
J. Paygod, Herts. 1389. (C.P. 40, 513, m. 37.)
J. Merygodde, Shrops. 1514. (K.B. 29, 146, m. 16.)

God-

Walt. fil' Godlamb, Norf. 1203. (Cur. Reg. R.)
Walt. God Spere, Lancs. 1203. (Cur. Reg. R.)
W. Godbarn, Lincs. 1203. (Cur. Reg. R.)
Rob. Godeblod, Bucks. 1261. (Ass. R. 58, m. 14d.)
Gilb. Godknave, Bucks. 1261. (Ass. R. 58, m. 27d.)
W. Godword, Bucks. 1271. (Ass. R. 60, m. 25.)
Thom. Godman, Bucks. 1286. (Ass. R. 65, m. 36.)
Hen. Godsone, Berks. 1292. (G.D. 91, m. 1.)
W. Godfrend, Warw. 1294. (G.D. 95, m. 4.)
W. Godspede, Bucks. 1382. (C.P. 40, 486, m. 478d.)

Hog-

Ralph Hoggesot, Ess. 1247. (Ass. R. 56, m. 2d.)
Mich. de Hogsawe, Bucks. 1257. (Ass. R. 57, m. 4.)
Rob. de Hogeputte, Bucks. 1261. (Ass. R. 58, m. 20d.)
W. Hoggeback, Cumb. 1279. (Ass. R. 131, m. 1.)
Rob. Hoggespol, Bucks. 1286. (Ass. R. 65, m. 43.)
Rob. Hogeman, Bucks. 1286. (Ass. R. 65, m. 48.)
J. Hoggebody, Warw. 1294. (Ass. R. 963, m. 21.)
W. Hoggeheler, Bucks. 1409. (G.D. 6, m. 7.)

-horn.

Bricmer Belehorne, Hunts. 1086. (Dom. Bk.)
Gilb. Blouhorn, Lincs. 1275. (Hund. R.)
Thom. Barlyhorn, Warw. 1286. (K.B. 27, 101, m. 31d.)
Bened. Buckehorne, Suss. 1288. (Subs. Salzmann.)
Hug. attehorne, Hants. 1292. (G.D. 91, m. 3.)
Alice Proudhorn, Ess. 1297. (Coram Rege: Phillimore, p. 221.)
Steph. de Mortishorn, 1297. (*Ibid.*, p. 2.)
J. Chophorn, Ess. 1327. (G.D. 18a, m. 11.)
W. Gosehorn, Dev. 1328. (G.D. 120, m. 18d.)
J. de Tomenhorn, Staffs. 1332. (Subs.)

Ill-

Rog. Yllefoster, Lond. 1197. (Pipe R.)
Adam Illeweder, Cumb. 1279. (Ass. R. 131, m. 2d.)
Nich. Illeknave, Yorks. 1289. (K.B. 27, 118, m. 11.)
Eudo Illeblod, Westm. 1290. (G.D. 69, m. 3.)
J. Illefflessh, Yorks. 1329. (Fines.)

Kill-

Ric. Kileman, Bucks. 1228. (Ass. R. 54, m. 15d.)
J. Cullecuppe, Bucks. 1261. (Ass. R. 58, m. 21d.)
Nich. de Culpin, Bucks. 1271. (Ass. R. 60, m. 16.)
Hen. Cullebulloc, Beds. 1275. (Hund. R.)
W. Cullehar, Oxf. 1275. (Hund. R.)
J. Cullebere, Beds. 1286. (Cl. R.)
Hen. Kyllebygg, Oxf. 1292. (G.D. 91, m. 9.)
W. Kulledeuel, Leic. 1300. (Ass. R. 1316, m. 8.)
Ric. Cullewether, Warw. 1313. (K. B. 27, 212, m. 24.)
J. Cullecuppe, Warw. 1320. (K.B. 27, 241, m. 86d.)
Rob. Cullebef, Beds. 1321. (G.D. 1, m. 30d.)
Rob. Killebole, Leic. 1327. (Subs. 133/1, m. 8.)
J. Kulbull, Bucks, 1381. (G.D. 14, m. 19.)

Note: There are a great number of place-names with initial K, and the following modern surnames are all of local origin: Kilby, Kilbrick, Kilburne, Kilford, Kilham, Killick, Killmaster, Kilpack, Kilpin, and Kilshaw. Kill-beef, -bull or -bullock appear to be occupational, but cf. Dion. Couillebeuf, Hen. V. (Norm. R.)

Lick-

Geof. Lickefinger, Norf. 1205. (Cur. Reg. R.)
Adam Likkebuffet, Herts. 1289. (C.P. 40, 333, m. 186.)
W. Lykkedoust, Ess. 13th c. (Anc. D. C883.)
Gilb. Lykkespyte, Norf. 1289. (K.B. 27, 116, m. 19.)
Steph. Likespigot, Cumb. 1292. (Ass. R. 136, m. 57d.)
W. Lickberd, Norf. 1299. (Pat. R.)
Rob. Lykkeloue, Northants. 1334. (Ass. R. 1400, m. 87d.)

Make-

W. Makeblith, Yorks. 1208. (Cur. Reg. R.)
Julian Makeblise, Oxf. 1275. (Hund. R.)
W. Makeblythe, Oxf. 1275. (Hund. R.)
Agnes Makewo, Hunts. 1286. (Ass. R. 345, m. 10d.)
Pet. Makemayden, Norf. 1288. (K.B. 27, 112, m. 23.)
W. Makejoye, Oxf. 1295. (G.D. 96, m. 28.)
Maud Makematte, Ess. 1289. (G.D. 18a, m. 29.)
W. Makenoise, Suff. 1299. (Ass. R. 1311, m. 100.)
W. Makepays, Northants. 1302. (G.D. 101, m. 10.)
J. Makepappe, Northants. 1313. (K.B. 27, 211, m. 92d.)
J. Makeman, Suff. 1333. (G.D. 64, m. 4.)
Mariota Makhayt, Cambs. 1352. (G.D. 136, m. 1.)
Agnes Makorneys, Ess. 1372. (C.P. 40, 441, 509d.)
W. Makfayre, Northumb. 1375. (G.D. 165a, m. 7d.)
J. Makelayke, Yorks. 1379. (Poll Tax, vii, 181.)
Walter Makeclerk, apprentice, Herts. 1428. (C.P. 40, 671, m. 553d.)

-nail.

W. Tingenail, Norf. 1204. (Cur. Reg. R.)
W. Horseneyl, Bucks. 1241. (Ass. R. 55, m. 20.)
Almaric de Vernayl, Berks. 1291. (G.D. 89, m. 10.)
Rob. Horsnayl, Berks. 1294. (G.D. 96, m. 6.)
Joan Tywarnayl, Corn. 1327. (Subs. 87/7, m. 7.)
Edw. Cartnayle, Surr. 1605. (K.B. 9, 717, no. 396.)

-pas. Ric. Noblepas, Staffs. 1202. (Cur. Reg. R.)
Ric. Marchepais, Dev. 1206. (Cur. Reg. R.)
Phil. Petypas, Warw. 1296. (G.D. 96, m. 38.)
J. Smalpas, Berks. 1297. (G.D. 96, m. 45.)
J. Taillepas, Ire. 1302. (Just. R.)
J. Geypas, Suff. 1357. (Cor. R. 177, m. 1.)
J. Malepas, Northants. 1373. (G.D. 152, m. 54.)
Adam Kypas, Yorks. 1379. (Poll Tax, vi, 2.)
W. Jolypas, Notts. 1380. (C.P. 40, 477, m. 252d.)
J. Horspas, Warw. 1403. (Ass. R. 1514, m. 40d.)
Sim. Manypas, Lond. 1432. (K.B. 29, 91, Hil. 10 Hen. 6.)
Note: This element is usually local, as in Malpas, the bad pass, but sometimes may signify 'step', cf. W. Stepwrong, Berks. 1175. (Pipe R.)

Sharp- W. Sharpspere, Kent, 1278. (Cl. R.)
W. de Sharpesawe, Staffs. 1333. (E179, 177/2, m. 9.)
Rob. Sharparowe, Yorks. 1379. (Poll Tax, p. 228.)
Rob. Sharpharowe, Cumb. 1502. (K.B. 29, 139, Mich. 18 Hen. 7.)
J. Sharpclyff, Staffs. 1503. (K.B. 29, 139, East. 18 Hen. 7.)
Walt. Sharpfurrowe, Surr. 1601. (K.B. 9, 709, no. 311.)

Spill- Spilman, Wilts.? 11th cent. (Shaftesbury Rental.)
Hen. Spilewyn, Bucks. 1247. (Ass. R. 56, m. 37d.)
Nigel Spillespon, Bucks. 1247. (Ass. R. 56, m. 47d.)
Eustace Spileman, Oxf. 1275. (Hund. R.)
Rog. Spillemalt, Oxf. 1280. (K.B. 27, 57, m. 5d.)
Thom. Spilepaternostr, Suff. 1284. (K.B. 27, 81, m. 1.)
Alan Spillale, Lincs. 1316. (K.B. 27, 224, m. 14.)
Steph. Spillebotere, Norf. 1318. (K.B. 27, 232, m. 62d.)
W. Spillepenny, Leic. 1326. (Ass. R. 470, m. 3.)
W. Spylcok, Ess. 1344. (C.P. 40, 333, m. 238.)
Ad. Spilgild or Spyllegille, Cumb. 1292. (Ass. R. 136, mm. 21, 52d.)
J. Spilewind, Suff. 1327. (Subs.)
Thom. Spilbrede, Cumb. 1350. (Pat. R.)
Rog. Spilfot, Norf. 1351. (Pat. R.)
J. Spilletymber, Suff. 1369. (S.C. 2, 203/59, m. 6.)

-tail.

J. Wrangetail, Herts. 1278. (Ass. R. 323, m. 46d.)
Gilb. Curtayl, Cumb. 1279. (Ass. R. 131, m. 3.)
Ad. Doggetayl, Warw. 1286. (Ass. R. 1272, m. 16.)
Ralph Haretayl, Lancs. 1288. (K.B. 27, 114, m. 38.)
Ric. Craketayl, Berks. 1294. (G.D. 95, m. 10.)
Isab. Grantayl, Berks. 1295. (G.D. 96, m. 21d.)
Walt. Cokkestail, Bucks. 1303. (K.B. 29, 15, m. 20.)
Hugh Doggetail, Worc. 1327. (Subs.)
Cath. Trewetail, Cambs. 1374. (G.D. 152, m. 46d.)
W. Shepestayll, Kent, 1411. (K.B. 9, 200, no. 42.)
Note: There was a place called Cattestayles in Wroxall, Warw. (Ryland, p. 36). Shepestayll had some connection with Sheppey, and is probably local as Sheepshead.

Thick-

Ric. de Thykethornes, Bucks. 1271. (Ass. R. 60, m. 34.)
Ralph de Thykness, Staffs. 1279. (Ass. R. Divers Co.)
Ric. de Thikebroom of Thikebroom, Staffs. 1473. (K.B. 9, 337, no. 6.)
J. Thikpeny, Yorks. 1486–7. (Surt. Soc., xcvi, p. 211.)

-water.

J. Ludewater, Bucks. 1261. (Ass. R. 58, m. 21.)
Mat. Attewater, Bucks. 1261. (Ass. R. 58, m. 27d.)
W. Aldewater, Bucks. 1269. (Ass. R. 59, m. 4d.)
Aug'tine Spurnewater, Norf. 1274. (Cl. R.)
J. Drinkwater, Shrops. 1275. (Hund. R.)
Thom. de Derewentewater, Cumb. 1278. (Ass. R. 130, m. 12.)
J. Underwater, Suff. 1283. (K.B. 27, 75, m. 14.)
Rob. de Bradewater, Bucks. 1286. (Ass. R. 65, m. 37d.)
Rob. Spyllewater, Warw. 1296. (G.D. 96, m. 29d.)
W. Warmwater, Salop, 1302. (K.B. 27, 167, m. 13d.)
Ric. Petiwater de Brightlyngeseye, 1342. (K.B. 29, 5, m. 76d.)
W. Coldwatur, Bucks. 1382. (G.D.14, m.7.)
Thom. Brynwater, —, 1460. (K.B.29, m.1.)

CHAPTER XIII

SOURCES AND LITERATURE

Lists of Names. The student intending to make original research into the roots of surnames will find excellent material in the indexes to the several hundred printed volumes of early records compiled by the Royal Commission and Public Record Office. Further valuable lists are provided by the printed transcripts of parish registers, will calendars, and various classes of documents, such as fines, subsidy rolls, etc. published by antiquarian societies.[1] Nowadays there is no lack of reliable material in print, the most convenient form for rapid scrutiny, nevertheless the investigator with plenty of time would be well advised to search original documents[2] of which a large collection is housed in the British Museum and the Public Record Office, as he can select classes of archives, which contain most names of the lower orders, and consequently more native appellatives, with moreover, a better chance of discovering that important factor the original habitat.

[1] In the event of using printed lists, only the most authoritative should be considered, as inexperienced transcribers make sad blunders; thus F. A. Inderwick, Q.C. (*Side-Lights on the Stuarts*, 1888, pp. 190–4) gave the following:—Pellacki for Sellack, Slade for Blake, Bruen for Gewen, Helbert for Edward, Knippe for Guppie, Clarkson for Glasson, Daye for Braye, Knumerton for Grimmerton, Hengler for Langley, Ypiana for Christiana, Farrier for Carrier, Anselbe for Andrews, Day for Guy, Corbett for Bovett, and Grantly for Traull, and numerous minor misreadings.

[2] The preserved documents, strictly speaking, are not original, but fair copies from an earlier draft, and there is reason to believe, often Latin translations from the French.

Manorial rolls are particularly valuable in this respect, the small tenants remaining in the same place for centuries, and Gaol Delivery and Pardon rolls may be recommended for the number of aliases given, they often providing valuable clues. Sometimes duplicate rolls can be found, as in the Assize class, and these are particularly instructive, since being copied by different recorders from a common draft, they may show considerable variation.

The student should not attempt to treat the subject entirely with the rigidity of an academician, but rather endeavour to understand the orthographic idiosyncrasies of the medieval clerk, remembering that the names were either taken down from dictation, or perhaps copied from a rough and hurried draft. Sometimes the scribe has a penchant for wrongly inserting the article *le*, others are too fond of the letter H for the modern taste, one clerk under Cornish influence, may use terminal *a* for *e*, as Whita, Bonda, Greya, Bata, Shorta, etc. (Dev. Subs. R. 1327), another preserve the ancient termination *n*, as Thomen, Hobben, Emmen, for Thomes, Hobbes, Emmes (Glouc. Subs. 1327), and yet another delighted to twist a name to make it amusing for his readers. In 1509, to give full effect to a certain pardon, necessitated enrolling the following aliases:—Aylnoth, Aynoth, Ayloff, Ayluff, Alluff, Ayloth, Aylwyn, Alwyn, Ayleff, Aylyff, or Aylnouth. More than philology would be essential to identify such variants when found on independent indictments, or to say whether Aylwin, Ayloff, or Aylnoth represented the original.

Authorities. There is no lack of literature on the subject of names. So long ago as 1603, the eminent antiquary William Camden, Clarenceux, published an essay in *Remaines concerning Britain*, which, without being scientific, gave a number of interesting facts, and expressed some quite sound views. Nothing further of much importance appeared until the middle of the nineteenth century, when several writers entered the field. M. A. Lower, a Sussex antiquary, compiled a volume on English Surnames and saw three editions appear, 1842-9, without any rivalry. These books contain a lot of amusing tittle-tattle, and many ill-digested examples, but used with caution, may yet sometimes provide a clue to origin. The third edition, much enlarged, added an index of 5,000 names. In 1857, an American, W. Arthur, published the first dictionary of names, soon, however, to be superseded by Lower's *Patronymica Britannica*, 1860, an alphabetical melange, containing a lot of interesting facts, interspersed with shocking bad guesses, such as Rigmaiden, 'a romping girl', and Thickness, from the 'thick nose of the bearer'! Both names are palpably derived from localities.

Robert Ferguson presented two works, in 1858 and 1864 respectively, in an endeavour to treat the subject scientifically, but in strongly stressing the Teutonic and Scandinavian origin of English names, he overdid his subject, even deriving the ancient Welsh Owen from Norse! As an example of the heights of imagination to which Ferguson could attain, reference may be made to Barnacle, "a surname or nickname given to a celebrated Norwegian pirate, who setting his face against the then fashionable amusement of tossing children on spears, was christened by his companions, to show their sense of his odd scruples, Barnakarl, 'baby's old man'." The name is of the local class, *e.g.* W. de Bernangle, Warw. 1331 (Ass. R. 1408, m. 3.), if not Vernicle!

The method of these authors was to collect names from current directories and guess the origin, no attempt being made to provide a chronological series running back to the earliest form. The pioneer step in citing sources is to the credit of C. W. Bardsley with *English Surnames*, which book, first appearing in 1873, ran through five editions with no material alterations, the last being in 1897. Six or seven thousand references to printed records, with numerous explanatory quotations from ME. literature are supplied. The volume, although a real advance, is replete with erroneous derivations, the author following the line of least resistance, taking names at their face value, with a fatal disregard for early proof. The success of Bardsley revived the interest of Lower, who without any marked revision, published a fourth edition of his *English Surnames*, in 1875; and of Ferguson, who designed a new work, *Surnames as a Science*, 1883, following the lines of his other essays, and regarding the subject mainly from the Teutonic standpoint, but he rightly expressed the view that many names are entirely different from what they appear to the modern eye; although it seems rather unwarranted to derive Archer, Boatwright, Mariner, and Plowman, from Teutonic personal names, on nothing more than conjecture. Of all these books Bardsley's are the most satisfying because of the dated, localised, and documented examples, and his *Dictionary*, on the same lines, which, commenced in 1866, appeared posthumously in 1901 is yet, for that reason by far the most valuable volume on *English* surnames. Although of great utility, this latter book is by no means conclusive, because the compiler made little or no use of any records of earlier date than the Hundred Rolls (c. 1275), and therefore the evidence of the two most valuable centuries is wanting. The result is a structure without foundation, many Old English survivals being overlooked, leading the compiler to class erroneously hundreds of appellatives as nicknames. He paid little or no attention to Welsh or Cornish origins, *Henn* to him being 'one who was hen-pecked'; he took no notice of alien influence, *Liquorish* was a nickname, not a corruption of the Jewish Licoricia, and he did not deal with Scottish and Irish surnames at all.

H. Harrison's *Dictionary* (1912) covers a more extensive field, making a strong feature of the etymology of words and local names, but, providing little evidence of the origin and employment of the names, should be used in conjunction with Bardsley. A book on novel lines was H. P. Guppy's *Homes of Family Names* (1890) in which the author expended great trouble in endeavouring to show the districts from which each name came, but his search being of necessity limited renders the result inconclusive.

Twentieth-century writers S. Baring-Gould, E. Weekley, and W. D. Bowman have cultivated the 'popular reader' style, grouping names under such intriguing captions as Vegetables, Flowers, Whiskers, and so on, only the most entertaining points being elaborated, and consequently a very small part of the subject comes under adequate review. These modern works barely touch Cornish, Welsh, Scottish and Irish names, and further fail in practical utility because they have no list of matters, few comparative examples are given, and any references to Patent, Close, or Pipe Rolls, etc., being undated, lead nowhere. From the want of systematic treatment derivations are often unacceptable, many being obviously unsound, for instance, Weekley presents such weird examples, as Anstey, 'a metronymic from Anastasia'! Pankhurst from Pentecost! Barefoot still serving duty as a nickname! Metcalf for mead calf! All four must be held to be local until disproved.

The want of a comprehensive survey led the present writer, in 1931, to compile *A History of Surnames of the British Isles*, which approaches the subject from the historical, etymological, and legal stand-point, and it is hoped, notwithstanding shortcomings, makes a first step towards placing the study of English onomatology on a sound basis. In that work (pp. 429–36) will be found a bibliography of 160 of the most useful books, the following being a short selection recommended for a first study.

BARDSLEY (C. W.) *A Dictionary of English and Welsh Surnames*, 1901.
EWEN (C. L.) *A History of Surnames of the British Isles*, 1931.
FORSSNER (Th.) *Germanic Names in England*, 1916.
HARRISON (H.) *Surnames of the United Kingdom*, 1912–8.
MOORE (A. W.) *Manx Names*, 1903.
REDIN (M.) *Studies on Uncompounded Personal Names*, 1919.
SEARLE (W. G.) *Onomasticon Anglo-Saxonicum*, 1897.
WOULFE (P.) *Sloinnte Gaedhael is Gall*, 1923.

The most valuable of the works dealing with foreign names are those by:—Dauzat (A.), French; Fick (F.C.A.), Greek, Sanskrit, etc.; Försteman (E.W.), Old German; Kalbow (W.), Old French; Van Hoorebeke (G.), Flemish; Larchey (L.), French; Leite de Vasconcellos (J.), Portuguese; Michaëlsson (K.), French; Nielsen (O.), Danish; Socin (A.), Middle High German; and Winkler (J.), Dutch.

INDEX OF NAMES AND ELEMENTS

INDEX OF NAMES AND ELEMENTS

Reference should also be made to the entries of first and second elements.